# POGUE'S
# BASICS:
# LIFE

Also by David Pogue:

*Pogue's Basics: Tech*
*Windows 10: The Missing Manual*
*OS X: The Missing Manual*
*iPhone: The Missing Manual*
*iPad: The Missing Manual*
*The World According to Twitter*
*Abby Carnelia's One and Only Magical Power*

# POGUE'S BASICS: LIFE

Essential Tips and Shortcuts
(That No One Bothers to Tell You)
for Simplifying Your Day

----------------------------------

## DAVID POGUE

FLATIRON
BOOKS

POGUE'S BASICS: LIFE. Copyright © 2015 by David Pogue. All rights reserved. Printed in the United States of America. For information, address Flatiron Books, 175 Fifth Avenue, New York, N.Y. 10010.

www.flatironbooks.com

The Library of Congress Cataloging-in-Publication Data is available upon request.

ISBN 978-1-250-08043-1 (trade paperback)
ISBN 978-1-250-08049-3 (e-book)

Our books may be purchased in bulk for promotional, educational, or business use. Please contact your local bookseller or the Macmillan Corporate and Premium Sales Department at 1-800-221-7945, extension 5442, or by e-mail at MacmillanSpecialMarkets@macmillan.com.

First Edition: November 2015

10 9 8 7 6 5 4 3 2 1

For the people who've taught me
all of life's basics:
Nicki, Kell, Tia, Jeff,
Jan, Cindy, Mom,
and Twitter

# Contents

--------------------

# POGUE'S BASICS: LIFE

# Introduction

I t takes time to get good at anything. Think how many years it takes people to become expert heart surgeons, cake bakers, or banjo players.

During your studies, teachers pass on to you what they've learned in their years of training, and you make occasional tiny discoveries of your own. Over time, on your way to mastery, you accumulate a lifetime of little tips, shortcuts, and essentials.

Well, guess what? There's just as much art to daily life as there is to heart surgery or banjo playing. But for *daily life,* there's no basic training course, no driver's ed. Food, health, clothing, traveling, shopping, socializing, setting up your home—each of these is a critical skill that you're somehow supposed to pick up on your own.

The people who are really good at them have spent years attaining that mastery. But very few are equally good at *all* of them.

This book's mission is to collect, in one place, all of those essential life techniques that your forefathers and foremothers have spent lifetimes discovering.

Did you know, for example, that on a highway sign, you can tell in advance which side of the road the exit ramp will be on—by which side of the sign the *exit number* is on?

*Exit will be on the left.* *Exit will be on the right.*

And did you know that if your ketchup is stuck in the bottle, you can get it flowing by swinging your arm in a circle?

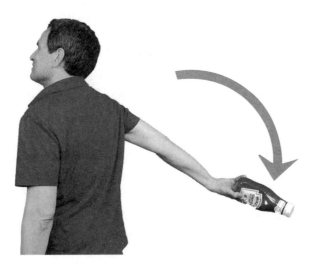

How about those times when you don't have your reading glasses? If you peek through a tiny hole you make with your fingers, you'll be astonished to discover that you can suddenly read small type without the glasses.

That's the kind of thing we're talking about: the little tips, tricks, and shortcuts of life. The surprising little payoffs of science in your everyday operations. The common knowledge that's not as common as you might think.

You may know some of these tips already. No problem; skim them and savor the rosy glow of smug superiority.

But more often, you'll probably realize that there are things you could be doing just a little bit better—to save time, money, and hassle.

## The birth of this book

Throughout my career as a writer of how-to technology books, I've spotted people using their gadgets wrong. Taking clumsy, roundabout ways to do things.

Often, I haven't been able to keep my mouth shut. I've stepped forward, invading the privacy of these total strangers, and showed them the better way.

But over time, I've become aware that it's not people's *fault* that they're clueless about tech. After all, there's no required course called Cell Phone 101. You can't sign up for Introduction to the Modern Tablet. Nobody goes through Email Boot Camp. How *are* people supposed to know about the essential techniques that make these things delightful?

In 2013, I put together my favorite ten tech tips and demonstrated them live onstage at the TED conference (a trendy annual gathering dedicated to Technology, Entertainment, and Design). The TED people posted the video of that talk on ted. com.

Four and a half million views later, I was convinced that I was on to something. So I wrote a whole book of these things— *Pogue's Basics: Tech.*

And guess what? *New York Times* best-seller list! TV appearances! A hug from my editor!

But wait a second. Why stop at technology?

The world is filled with activities, processes, and skills that we've all had to pick up, randomly and untutored. Traveling, cooking, clothing, shopping, driving, staying healthy....Why shouldn't someone round up all the *life* tips demonstrated by experts at these things?

So here you have it: *Pogue's Basics: Life.* A sequel that opens up the scope somewhat but embraces the same philosophy: "Here are the most important tricks to know—the ones that you probably assume *everyone* knows, but they don't."

If you pick up only *one new trick* from these pages that makes your life easier...

Well, then it wasn't a very good book.

But you'll probably pick up a lot more than that.

## What this book doesn't cover

"Oh," people say. "You mean you're writing a book of life hacks?"

The Internet teems with Web sites and forwarded emails filled with what have become known as *life hacks*. In principle, a life hack is just what this book promises: a little clever tip or trick that makes life easier.

In practice, though, most of the passed-around Internet hacks are disappointing or useless for these reasons:

- **They don't work at all.** "If you reheat leftover pizza together with a glass of water in the microwave, the crust comes out crisp." It actually doesn't. At all. (Why would it? Mushy crust comes from *too much* moisture, not *not enough*.)

- **They're tacky.** "You can amplify your smartphone's speaker by inserting it into an empty cardboard toilet paper tube." Are you really going to put your phone into a toilet paper roll? No, you are not.

- **They're ridiculously obvious.** "To prevent bottles of liquid from spilling when you travel, put them into sealed plastic bags." Really?!

- **They're dumb.** "In a pinch, you can use Doritos as kindling to start a campfire." I'm not making this up.

Other tips that aren't in this book: techniques that work only for some people, some of the time ("To get rid of hiccups, put a penny between your toes"). Tips that would be hard to prove ("You get better ideas if you hold meetings during outdoor walks"). Tips that are good, common-sense models for living but aren't especially surprising ("A friendly smile will get you better service from a waiter or clerk").

Instead, the morsels in this book describe features hidden right under our noses, features that lots of people don't know about. As well as "Everyone's been using it wrong" insights. Plus tips that are clever, unexpected, and *useful*.

And—and this is a big "and"—all of them work. You can't believe how much time my team and I have spent in kitchens, cars, and laundry rooms, testing these tips to make sure they do what they're supposed to.

Along those lines, I should mention that, frankly, I'm a lot better at technology than I am at daily life. So I've had help with this book. My brilliant wife, Nicki; my ingenious mom; and trusted friends Jan Carpenter and Cindy Love all contributed their wisdom (and helped me test the submissions of others).

I also asked my Twitter followers to share their own hard-won life tips. You'll find some of their contributions in these pages, too, with credit. (I've also sent each contributor a signed copy of this book.)

But enough preamble. Let the Basics begin!

# Chapter 1: **The Car**

Ah, the car. A two-ton machine made of 30,000 parts. Millions upon millions of earthlings buy them, operate them, or maintain them every hour of every day.

In other words, it's pretty unlikely that you know everything important there is to know about your auto—yet.

---

## The air-conditioning question, answered at last

"Chris, close the window. I'm going to turn on the air conditioning."

"No, don't do that! The AC uses up more gas!"

"I know, but it uses *less* gas than driving with the window open. The wind resistance means it's harder to push the car through the air, so we use more fuel."

How many times a year is this argument replayed in cars these days?

According to the Society of Automotive Engineers, the air conditioner uses less fuel. (Driving with the windows open imposes a 20 percent gas penalty; the air conditioner, only 10 percent.)

The exception: slow driving. Under 40 miles per hour, open windows introduce very little additional drag on the car. So in that case, opening the windows is slightly more fuel-efficient than running the air conditioner.

In other words, you're *both* sort of right.

-----------------------------------------------

# The secret meaning in highway exit signs

This is an exposé of those standard green American highway signs—specifically, the ones that announce an upcoming *exit*.

Above the sign, you generally see a small, additional sign bearing the upcoming exit's *number* (EXIT 3, for example).

That number sign is silently communicating *which side* of the highway the exit ramp will be on. If the smaller sign is on the *left* side of the larger sign, the exit will be on the left; if it's on the right, it'll be on the right.

Cool, huh?

# The gas-tank indicator you didn't know was there

When you pull up at a gas station, it's helpful to know which *side* of your car the fuel tank is on. That piece of information determines how you pull into the gas-pump islands.

You probably know by now whether *your* car's gas cap is on the left or right side. But what if you're driving a rental, or you're driving someone else's car, or you've just bought a *new* car? In those situations, it's worth knowing about the handy triangle on the fuel gauge of every single car.

See the arrow? It points to the side of the car your gas tank is on!

# Unlock all the car doors remotely

Most new cars can be unlocked remotely by pressing the unlock button on the key fob. Handy.

But that button generally unlocks only the *driver's* door. What if other people are trying to get into the car simultaneously—your spouse, your boss, your clients, your kids—and it's freezing cold or pouring rain?

**WRONG:** Unlock the driver's side door. Open it. Get in. Hunt for the unlock button on the driver's door armrest. Look like a self-absorbed jerk.

**RIGHT:** Press the unlock button on your key fob *twice.* That unlocks *all* of your car's doors simultaneously.

# Extend your key fob's wireless range

This one sounds so preposterous, it will surely strike you as nonsense—but it really works.

When you hold your car's remote control *against your head,* you can lock and unlock your doors from much farther away. Depending on the car model and your body composition, you may gain as much as 90 feet of range (about six car lengths).

When this tip is passed around online, people usually suggest holding the fob under your chin. But you'll probably find that something fleshy, like your cheek, works better than something bony.

That's because behind the scenes—or, rather, inside the scenes—the fluids of your head act as a conductor. Your body becomes part of the antenna—a much bigger one. If you're old enough to remember when TV sets had rabbit-ear antennas, you may recall that you sometimes got the clearest picture when you were touching the antenna. Same principle here.

Now, if only the same thing worked for extending the range of our *cell phones*....

---

# Nail polish to ID different keys

There once were two really dumb cowboys. They had a terrible time telling their horses apart.

They tried trimming one horse's tail, but it soon grew back. They tried nicking one horse's ear, but the other horse accidentally nicked its ear in the same place.

Finally, in desperation, they *measured* the two horses. And they discovered that, sure enough, the black horse was two inches taller than the white one.

And with that background, you now see the logic of this trick: You can use nail polish to color-code the heads of the keys on your key ring. Nail polish is bright, it's distinct, and it lasts a long time. And it saves you from fumbling if you have more than one car key (or house key).

# The self-pumping gas nozzle

You know how to pump gas into your car, right? Of course you do. You open the little panel in the side of your car, unscrew the gas cap, insert the hose nozzle, and squeeze the handle. Then you stand there, freezing (Buffalo), boiling (Atlanta), or getting rained upon (Seattle), until your tank is full and the handle clicks and shuts off.

There's a better way. Maybe you know this; maybe you don't: On most pumps, you can *lock* the nozzle handle in the ON position, so that you don't have to squeeze it or even touch it. Look for the little metal tongue on the inside of the handle. It flips down into the lower part of the handle and gets propped there.

Once you've locked the nozzle, you can walk away. You can get back into your car or run into the convenience store for a coffee. When your tank is full, the pump stops pumping automatically, and you can withdraw the nozzle as usual.

# How not to be blinded by oncoming headlights

It's nighttime. You're on some two-lane road, maybe without streetlights. Cars coming toward you have their headlights on, of course—and if you're not careful, they'll make you lose your night vision. Especially if the guy coming toward you has his brights on.

The solution: Focus on the white line at the right side of *your* lane. (There's a handy rhyme to help you remember: "Look at the white on the right if there's too much light.")

You'll be able to stay in your lane without being blinded by the oncomers.

# An essay on windshield defogging

Frost on the outside of the windshield isn't the only bad thing that can happen in cold weather. Fog on the *inside* is bad, too.

Defogging a windshield is simple, but it's really counterintuitive unless you know why the fog is there.

Why does the moisture—condensation—build up on the inside of the glass? Because your body heat and breath are making the air inside the car *warm and moist,* yet the air outside the car is *cold and dry.* The vapor from your breath lands on the inside of the cold windshield and turns into a fine mist.

You can't do much to change the cold, dry weather outside. But you *can* make the inside air less warm and wet.

- **First, draw in fresh air.** Your first thought should be about the Recirc control. Switch it so that rather than recirculating the air, your car is drawing dry air into the car from outside. (It might be either a button or a sliding lever.)

That may seem odd, since it's *cold* outside and you're trying to warm up your body. But if you just recirculate the warm, wet air, you won't defog the windows.

(If you're in a hurry, opening the windows is a *really* fast way to get cold, dry air into the car—which will defog the windows. It's also uncomfortable and noisy.)

- **Second, turn on Defrost full blast—and the AC, too.** The Defrost control blows hot air onto the glass to warm it up, so it'll stop condensing water vapor. (Yes, the control is called Defrost, which is different from *defogging*. But in both cases, you want hot air blowing on the glass.)

On most cars, turning on Defrost automatically turns on the air conditioner. If it doesn't, turn on the AC manually at this point.

This is the counterintuitive part. Why would you turn on the AC in the winter? As it turns out, you're not running the AC to make the air *colder*; you're running it to make the air *drier,* so there will be less vapor to condense. (Yes, the air conditioner has that effect.) In fact, you can turn the *temperature* of the AC all the way to hot if you want.

This step produces a one-two punch: It makes the interior air drier with the air conditioner, and it makes the windshield warmer with the Defrost blower.

Incidentally, the opposite effect can happen in hot weather (this means you, Florida): Condensation can form on the *outside* of the glass. Your air conditioner has made it cool and dry *inside,* and it's hot and humid outside.

The solution? Run your wipers, or give the AC a rest.

--------------------------------------------------------

# A treatise on windshield frost

In cold weather, frost may develop on your windshield. In general, driving without being able to see out the windshield is undesirable.

Every car has a feature designed to melt that ice: the Defrost button. It looks like this:

It works by blowing warm air on your windshield. Since it's blowing from the *inside* of the glass, it takes a while to melt the frost on the *outside.* You can use your wipers and wiper fluid to hurry things along, but it's still not speedy.

That's why the world has come up with better ways of defrosting:

- **Pour warm water onto the windshield** (the outside) to melt whatever's there; it then wipes away with a quick wipe of your wipers. (Don't use *hot* water; a drastic temperature change could crack the glass.)

- **If the ice has built up,** use a plastic ice scraper; if you don't have one and you're desperate, you can use the long edge of a credit card.

Incidentally: If you *anticipate* snow or ice, you can throw a towel across the windshield the night before, to collect the snow and insulate the glass from ice. Pin it in place with your wipers. That'll make life a *lot* easier in the morning.

------------------------------------------------

# Your car should have a trash can

It's unbelievable that *trash containers* aren't standard elements of every car. Every driver ingests scraps of stuff to throw away: food wrappers, receipts, flyers, parking tickets. (Joke! That's a joke.)

You can, of course, buy an actual car trash bag that hangs behind the headrest. (Yes, they sell those.) You can use a plastic bag over the headrest, too.

Or you can use one of those clear plastic pouring bins that usually store cereal, with or without the lid.

But the point is, outfit your car with *something*. Otherwise, it won't be long until your floor mats are a fire hazard/gerbil nest.

------------------------------------------------

# How to get text messages without crashing

Reading or typing on your phone behind the wheel is *insanely* dangerous; it's exactly as safe as driving with your eyes closed.

What's that you say? "Everyone knows that"?

Then why are 40 percent of car accidents today caused by drivers with phones in their hands? And why do 27 percent of all adults (35 percent of teenagers) admit to having texted while driving in the past 30 days?

Here's a slightly safer idea: When you hear a text coming in, use Siri (on an iPhone). Hold down your iPhone's Home button while you say "Read my new messages." Your phone reads them *aloud,* so you can judge whether or not they're important enough to justify pulling over and stopping your car.

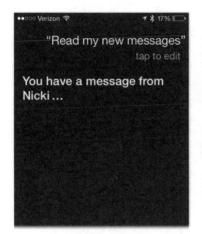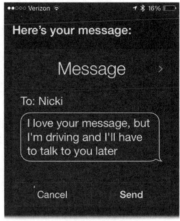

Siri then invites you to dictate a reply—again, without ever taking your eyes off the road or your hands off the wheel.

If you have an Android phone, you can download an app that gives you the same kind of feature. ReadItToMe, for example, is free.

# The correct pressure for your tires

You might have been told, as a wee lad/lass, that there's a number molded into the side of your car's tires, specifying the correct tire pressure.

You've been misled. There *is* a number on your tire's sidewall, but it's the *maximum* inflation pressure, not the *desired* pressure.

To find out the *best* pressure for your tires, look for a sticker inside the driver's-side door frame, usually stuck on sideways. (It may also appear on a sticker in the glove compartment or in the user's manual.)

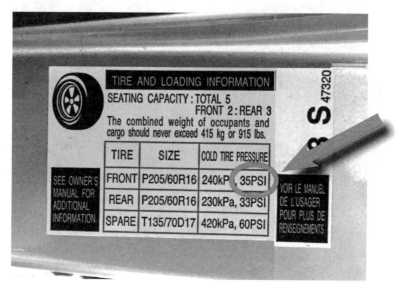

For cars, the best pressure is typically from 30 to 35 psi (pounds per square inch); for small trucks, it's 35 to 40. You take these measurements with a tire-pressure gauge; it's about $5 at a hardware store. There's usually one on the air pump at gas stations, where most people go to fill their tires.

Do your testing when the tires are cold—at least half an hour after their most recent long drive—because they heat up, increasing the pressure, when you drive.

The other thing to know about inflating your tires: A little more pressure gives you better fuel economy and less wear on the tires. Less pressure gives you better traction. You can't have both.

# Let your phone remember where you parked

These days, iPhones and Android phones can track your fitness, track your sleep, track your location—so why shouldn't they remember where you parked your car?

That's exactly the idea behind apps like Find My Car (free for iPhone or Android) or the easier-to-use Honk ($1 for iPhone) and Park Me Right (free for Android). They use GPS to remember where you parked—and to guide you back to the spot.

Beats wandering around through a vast landscape of cars, panicking and delaying your bedtime.

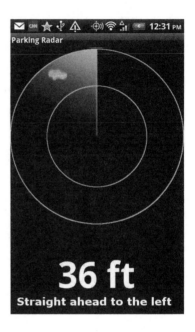

# How to buy a car

This is not your father's car-buying era. These days, when it comes to negotiating a car's price, the dealership no longer has the upper informational hand. Thanks to the Internet, you can know as much about the numbers as the dealership does. The research takes time and effort, but you can save a *lot* of money.

Here's the most effective way to get a good deal on a car:

- **Find out the dealer's invoice price for the exact car you want.** You can find out what the *dealer* paid for the car by looking it up at Edmunds.com or TrueCar.com.

   The truly savvy car shopper doesn't negotiate the car's price, but rather the *amount over or under that invoice price.*

   Of course, the dealer is entitled to make *some* profit. But often, there are numbers you're not seeing here, such as incentive payments from the car manufacturer. That's why a dealer may sometimes seem to be offering you a price that's actually *under* what he paid.

- **Let the dealerships compete.** Call a number of dealerships; ask for the "Internet sales manager" of each and for her email address. In your email, let her know that you're comparison shopping. Ask how much over or under the invoice price she's willing to offer you. Also ask what the final, out-the-door price will be.

   Compare the responses. Contact the dealership with the *worst* offer, tell it the *best* offer you got, and give it a chance to beat it. Work through the other offers this way.

   By the end of the process, you'll have a killer deal. You should be able to pull up at that dealership, sign the papers, and drive away.

---------------------------------------------------------------

# When to buy a car

Your ability to get a good deal on a car depends a lot on *when* you're buying it.

The timings of your dealer visit, salesperson meeting, and test drive don't matter. However, you should call the same salesperson *later* to make your offer—for best results, at one of these times:

- **Saturday or Sunday night, an hour before closing time.** Often, car dealerships will be eager to make one more deal before the week's end. Especially if they've had a bad week.

- **The last day of the month.** Same logic. Car dealerships earn bonuses if they meet certain sales goals each month. Your offer might be the one that pushes them over the brink.

- **A bad-weather day.** Terrible weather, like snow or rain, can really kill a dealership's sales. Salespeople might be especially eager to talk to you on days like this.

---

# How to get rid of your existing car

Just so you know: You'll *always* get more for your used car by selling it yourself, online. If you use it as a trade-in when buying a *new* car, the dealership's offer will be much lower. In effect, you're buying convenience.

How do you know what your used car is worth? You look it up in the Kelley Blue Book at kbb.com.

# Secrets of the VIN number (or, "How to tell what year a car was made")

Every car and truck made since 1980 has a VIN—a vehicle identification number, which is like the car's Social Security number. You can find it in lots of places: on a tiny plaque fastened to your dashboard, right up against the windshield on the driver's side; on a sticker inside the driver's door well; in the engine bay; on your insurance card; and on your car's registration papers.

The VIN is a mighty storehouse of encoded information about your car. Encrypted in those 17 digits, you can decipher information like the year of the car's manufacture, what kind of engine it contains, where it was built, and so on. You have to refer to the VIN if (a) your car is stolen, (b) you want to sell or register a car, (c) you take the car in for repairs (so that the shop can order the proper parts), (d) you're researching the history of a used car, or (e) you get sweaty palms when you contemplate storehouses of encoded information.

By far the easiest way to unravel the mysteries of your VIN is to visit www.VINDecoder.net. Type in your VIN, and presto: There are all the secrets it contains.

But what if you can't get online right now? What if you're reading this on a desert island, in a cheap hotel, or in the bathtub?

Then here's the key. Suppose your VIN number is JHMGE88639S021402. Here's how it breaks down:

- **J.** That's the country where the car was made. It's probably a 1, 4, or 5 (USA); 2 (Canada); 3 (Mexico); J (Japan); K (South Korea); S (England); W (Germany); or Y (Sweden or Finland). So far, we know this is a Japanese-made car.

- **H.** That's the manufacturer code. A for Audi, B for BMW, G for General Motors, H for Honda, L for Lincoln, N for Nissan, T for Toyota, and so on. The H in this example tells you "Honda."

- **M.** The third character designates the car's type or the car company's division. (Each car company makes up its own code system here.) In Honda's case, you'll see either an M (car, built in Japan), G (car, built in America), or L (multipurpose car). This one's a car built in Japan.

- **GE886.** The next five characters specify the car's model, body type, restraint system, transmission type, and engine. Each car company uses its own system to make up this code, and these code systems change every few years. In this case, we're looking at a four-door, front-wheel drive Honda Fit hatchback.

- **3.** This number is a checksum—a verification digit. It's derived by a math formula from all the *other* characters of the code and indicates right away whether or not this is a valid VIN.

- **9.** That's the car's model year. Your car was made in year 9.

Ha, fooled you—it's not that old! Actually, the 9 means 2009, according to this table:

| A—1980 | L—1990 | Y—2000 | A—2010 |
|--------|--------|--------|--------|
| B—1981 | M—1991 | 1—2001 | B—2011 |
| C—1982 | N—1992 | 2—2002 | C—2012 |
| D—1983 | P—1993 | 3—2003 | D—2013 |
| E—1984 | R—1994 | 4—2004 | E—2014 |
| F—1985 | S—1995 | 5—2005 | F—2015 |
| G—1986 | T—1996 | 6—2006 | G—2016 |
| H—1987 | V—1997 | 7—2007 | H—2017 |
| J—1988 | W—1998 | 8—2008 | J—2018 |
| K—1989 | X—1999 | 9—2009 | K—2019 |

After hours of study, it may occur to you that this table lists the alphabet letters (A, B, C) *twice*. The letter D seems to indicate either 1983 *or* 2013. You're correct; the car-industry elders decided that there was little chance of confusing two cars that are 30 years apart.

- **S.** This character lets you know which factory made the car. Each car company makes up its own codes for this slot. Honda has 11 plants all over the world; the S refers to the one in Suzuka, Mie, Japan.

- **021402.** This final string of six digits are a serial number for your car. In this case, our Honda Fit was the 21,402nd car manufactured at this particular plant.

# The old tennis-ball parking-position trick

If you (or your newly licensed teenager) seem to be having trouble stopping your car at exactly the right place in the garage each day, this is an oldie but goodie:

Hang a tennis ball on a string from the garage ceiling. Position it so that your windshield will just touch the ball when you pull the car into precisely the right spot.

That way, you'll never (a) crush the bicycles parked in front of you or (b) allow the garage door to chop off the back of the car.

# Don't use the engine as a brake

If you're going fast, or down a hill, you can slow the car by taking your foot off the gas. Since it's still in gear, the engine acts as a brake. Thus the clever name: engine braking. Trucks do it all the time.

In a car, though, you're better off just using the brakes. Both techniques put stress on the car. But it's a lot less expensive to buy new brake pads than a new transmission or clutch.

(As for the trucks: They're *designed* to engine-brake.)

# There's a logic to sign colors and shapes

The big red STOP sign! The bright yellow YIELD sign! So many pretty colors!

As it turns out, your government has put a lot of thought into those colors. They actually mean something. They're consistent. Here's your cheat sheet:

- Red always means "stop, or you'll crash." (DO NOT ENTER, STOP, WRONG WAY.)

- Orange is for temporary construction signs. (DETOUR, MEN AT WORK.)

- Yellow signs are advisory; they usually mean "caution." (YIELD, SLOW.)

- **Green** indicates directional information. (EXIT 23, BIKE ROUTE.)

- **Blue** is for traveler services. (FUEL, FOOD, LODGING, HOSPITAL, PARKING.)

- **Brown** describes points of interest. (SCENIC OVERLOOK, CAMPING.)

- **Black-and-white** signs are for regulations. (SPEED LIMIT, NO PARKING, ONE WAY.)

There's a logic to the shapes of signs, too. Round means "railroad"; triangle means "yield"; pentagon means "school"; diamond indicates potential hazards ahead; and a tall rectangle is for regulations—like NO PARKING and SPEED LIMIT.

--------------------------------------------------------

# Driving without dying: The Basics

If you're 16 or 17, you've probably taken driver's ed classes fairly recently, and you probably don't need a refresher.

If you're somewhat older, it might be worth reading a recap of what decades of research and science have established:

- **The three-second rule.** If you rear-end another car for any reason, the law will consider the accident your fault. You can avoid that outcome by using the three-second distance rule, which goes like this:

  Mentally choose a fixed point that's even with the car in front of you, such as a light pole or a sign. If *you* reach that point before you can count to "three-one-thousand," you're too close to the car in front of you. (You're supposed to *increase* that distance in dark or wet conditions.)

- **Stop-sign sequence.** When you and other drivers pull up at the same stop-sign intersection, it's not always clear who should go first. The answer is simple: First to stop = first to go. That is, whoever arrived at the intersection first gets to *go* first.

Well, that's pretty clear—until you pull up at your stop sign and discover a line of *four* cars already waiting in another lane. Cars 2, 3, and 4 were already waiting in line before you arrived. Don't they get to go before you?

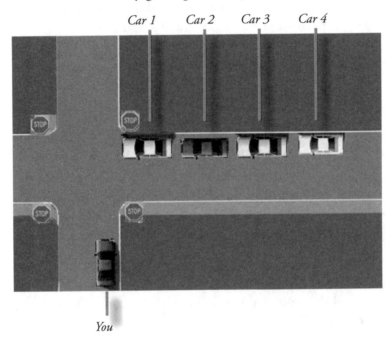

Nope. Because you arrived at the *intersection* before they did.

Oh—and if it's a tie, the car on the right gets to go first.

- **Emergency stops.** If you need to slam on the brakes, the technique varies depending on whether your car has ABS (anti-lock braking system) or not. Most recent cars do, and it's important to know if your car is among them. (How do you know? An indicator light, saying ABS or "Anti-Lock," comes on every time you start the car.)

  If you do have ABS, here's how to stop suddenly: Press hard on the brake. Period. It may pulsate violently, but don't fear. The pulsing is a result of your computerized brakes and their grabbing and releasing in rapid succession, which slows the car quickly without skidding.

  If your car *doesn't* have ABS, push the brake about 70 percent of the way down—stop short of letting the car skid. And don't turn the steering wheel very hard. Swerving *while* braking is a recipe for losing control.

- **Staying awake.** In a 2005 study, 37 percent of American drivers admitted to having fallen asleep behind the wheel during the year. Pretty scary to think that you're sharing your road with hurtling cars that have nobody in control.

  If you're drowsy, and there's no way to pull over for a nap somewhere, eat something. Make it last. Munch something tart, tangy, or minty. Eat an apple. Or suck a minty Tic Tac or, better yet, an Altoid. It's very hard to fall asleep with an Altoid in your mouth.

  Chewing gum works well, too, according to truck drivers, as long as you keep actually chewing.

  Another great trick: Listen to music you don't like—something as annoying as possible. (Music you *do* like can make you fall asleep *faster.*)

You can also annoy yourself awake by putting your seat back into an uncomfortable position. Drive with one hand in the air. Open the windows. Make your face wet. Run the air conditioner a little colder than you like it.

# Chapter 2: **Travel**

Our network of travel options has become one of the world's great wonders. You can get from anywhere to anywhere else, with a speed, price, and reliability that would have amazed our ancestors.

But our network of travel options has also become complex. Security, rules and regulations, and added charges can make huge dents in your comfort and mood.

Unless, of course, you know the rules of the road—and the sky.

---

## Meet arriving passengers at Departures

If your job is to pick up some *arriving* passengers at the airport, your first instinct is probably to greet them on the airport's *Arrivals* level (or area). It would be backward to meet them at Departures, right?

Yes. But the problem with arrivals is that *everyone else* is waiting to pick up passengers there, too. The Arrivals curb is usually a giant traffic jam, filled with idling cars. Most airports employ security guards to chase you away, forcing you to circle the airport again and again until your passengers finally emerge from the terminal.

But on the *Departures* level of the airport, there's no traffic jam. Cars pull up, discharge passengers, and drive away. There's plenty of space for you to pull up and wait—and in most cases, there are no guards yelling at you to circle the airport. Usually, you can wait comfortably at the curb until your loved ones arrive.

## Three Web sites for less agonizing air travel

These three Web sites give you juicy insight that will make you a lot more comfortable in flight. Bookmark 'em. Use 'em.

• **FlightAware.com.** Type in a flight number, and see where that flight is in the sky *at that second,* as well as its projected landing time. It's fantastic if you're supposed to pick someone up at the airport. You also get to see maps of its altitude and speed, the highest and lowest prices paid for tickets on that flight, and most useful of all: the flight number's record for being early or late.

- **SeatGuru.com.** Don't choose a seat online until you've looked it up on this site! You'll find out if your seat doesn't recline, doesn't have a window, has a broken TV, and so on. No ugly surprises.

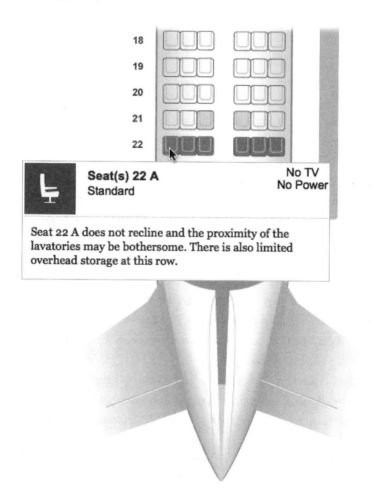

- **SeatAlert.com.** When you book your flight and find out that only middle seats are available, what should you do? Panic? No—go to this Web site and ask to be notified if an aisle or window opens up. They often do, so you can swoop in and snag them.

(Each of these sites also has a phone app that performs the same stunts. Ready, set, download!)

-------------------------------------------------------------------

# What the three-letter airport codes mean

Every airport on earth has a three-letter code. It's a great time-saving shorthand for pilots, baggage handlers, travel agents, and so on.

It's easy to understand why MIA means the Miami airport, BOS means Boston, and SLC is Salt Lake City. But it's not as easy to understand why Vancouver is YVR, Baltimore is BWI, and Chicago is ORD.

In the beginning, airports inherited the existing *two*-letter codes that the National Weather Service had been using for cities, such as LA for Los Angeles, PH for Phoenix, PD for Portland, Oregon. When the airport codes expanded to three letters, many just tacked on an *X* to fill out the abbreviation: LAX, PHX, PDX, and so on.

Sometimes, a city's former name solves the mystery. The airport in Beijing (formerly Peking) is known as PEK; St. Petersburg (formerly Leningrad) is LEN; Mumbai (formerly Bombay) is BOM.

Then there are airports named after an important local historical figure. Nashville's has BNA (for Col. Harry S. Berry);

Knoxville's is TYS (after Navy pilot Charles McGhee Tyson); and Spokane's is GEG (for Maj. Harold Geiger).

Or historical *airfields.* Orlando's airport (MCO) was once McCoy Air Force Base; Chicago's (ORD) is on the former Orchard Place; and New Orleans's airport (MSY) used to be the Moisant Stock Yards.

Complicating matters: Commercial airport codes can't begin with an *N*, since that letter belongs to Navy airports. Nor can they start with a *W* or a *K*, which are reserved for radio stations. Canada, meanwhile, has grabbed *Y* to designate *its* airports, such as YVR for Vancouver, YYC for Calgary, and YUL for Montreal.

OK, so you're not allowed to start your airport code with an *N*, a *W*, or a *K*. So what are you supposed to do if your city's name is Newark, Wilmington, or Key West?

You skip the first letter altogether. That's why Newark is EWR, Wilmington is ILM, and Key West is EWY.

Or you get creative. Washington National Airport can't use *W* or *N*, so it's DCA (District of Columbia Airport).

You'd think Dulles International Airport would be DIA, but when handwritten, it looks too much like the *other* Washington airport, DCA. So they spell it backward: IAD.

Once a code becomes known to the airplane industry, it's awfully hard to change. Just ask Sioux City, Iowa, whose airport abbreviation is, to this day, SUX.

---

# Cheap airfare: The Basics

The prices of airline tickets, as you may be aware, vary to an almost nonsensical degree.

Here's an example from FlightAware.com. A passenger who paid $54 for a coach ticket on this flight could be sitting right next to someone who was charged a princely $2,135:

**Non-stop fares**

Passengers traveling from SFO (San Francisco, CA) to JFK (New York, NY) paid the following amounts for that one-way ticket during the previous 12 months:

| Fare class | Minimum/Ticket | Maximum/Ticket | Revenue/Flight |
|---|---|---|---|
| Restricted Business Class | $250.07 | $2,405.24 | $1,086.02 |
| Restricted First Class | $162.92 | $2,361.54 | $1,243.41 |
| Restricted Coach Class | $54.05 | $2,135.00 | $40,762.76 |

Why the variation? The airlines have developed complicated software that offers different prices to different potential passengers at different times. Their interest is in computing the *highest* price you're likely to pay. They take into account the route, the time of day/week/year, your past spending on plane travel, the competition, and psychology.

If you do a Web search for "when to buy plane tickets," you'll be treated to a huge list of old wives' tales. One might tell you that tickets are lowest when you buy on Tuesdays, or lowest when you *fly* midweek, or lowest 52 days before the flight.

Are you sitting down? *None* of that is true.

Even the old Saturday Night Rule is rarely true anymore—the one that says if you can stay over on a Saturday night in your destination city, your round-trip fare will be lower.

These factors, however, *are* true:

- **When to buy.** Prices tend to go up in the month before the flight, peaking *immediately* before the flight. That's because business travelers are the ones most likely to book flights at the last minute—and they're the ones who can afford steep prices.

You generally won't save money by buying a ticket *more* than a month out, however. In fact, booking six months or a year in advance may cost you dearly, because in that time, your plans are likely to change.

- **Flexibility = money.** On flight-search Web sites such as Hipmunk.com, Travelocity.com, and Kayak.com, you can indicate that your travel dates are flexible. If you are, indeed, willing to shift your departure or return by a day or so, you can save big bucks, precisely because you're doubling or tripling your odds of finding a sweet spot in the airlines' complicated pricing structure.

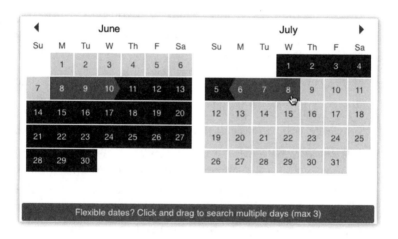

Those sites also let you specify flexibility in *airports*. Lots of cities are served by multiple airports: New York has JFK, LaGuardia, Newark, and even Islip (Long Island) and White Plains. Tell Hipmunk, Travelocity, or Kayak that you're willing to consider other airports—and here again, you multiply your odds of finding lower fares.

- **Don't forget Southwest.** Southwest Airlines is unique for a few reasons. First, it flies a lot of routes (in the Southwest, of course) that nobody else does. Second, it doesn't assign seats; it's first come, first served.

  Finally, Southwest doesn't share its flight-schedule data with the flight-search Web sites, such as Hipmunk and Kayak! Those sites never show you Southwest options; to see them, you have to go to Southwest's own Web site. Annoying, but true.

- **Consider "throwaway ticketing."** It may defy the laws of common sense—but it's often less expensive to buy a round-trip ticket than a one-way ticket! So if you need a one-way flight from, say, New York to Chicago, look up the round-trip price; it may be lower.

  If you buy such a ticket, go ahead and fly to Chicago. Just don't use the return ticket.

  However, you should call the airline a couple of hours before the flight to let them know you won't be aboard. For two reasons: First, you may get a refund (if it was a refundable ticket) or a credit for a future flight (if it was a non-refundable ticket). Second, it's good karma to let the airline give your seat to some poor soul who really needs it.

------------------------------------------------

# Get your next driver's license verified—or you won't fly

In the United States, a driver's license is fairly easy to forge; just ask any 16-year-old in a bar. And yet that license is considered good enough ID to let you onto plane flights! It's not, ahem, much of a barrier to terrorists.

Furthermore, every state issues its own kind of driver's license, which has its own requirements and design. It's not really a *national* ID card.

That's why, in 2005, Congress passed the Real ID act—and the *verified* driver's license was born. You can't get this kind of license without showing two *other* forms of government ID, such as a Social Security card and a birth certificate.

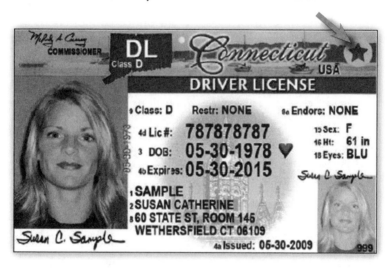

When your current license expires and it's time to renew, you'd be wise to get the verified type as its replacement. You have to do this in person, either at your state's Department of Motor Vehicles or a local AAA office. (The AAA will do the job for you even if you're not an AAA member.)

Why? According to the current timeline (which may change), starting in 2017, the old type of driver's license will no longer be accepted as ID at airports. If you want to get onto a plane, you'll have to show either a verified driver's license or a passport.

# Striking back against the toothpaste-industrial complex

As you probably know, the TSA doesn't let you travel with liquids or gels in containers that hold more than 3.4 ounces.

That's a goofy rule for a hundred reasons. For example, you're perfectly welcome to bring *three* 3.4-ounce containers of the same liquid. And they care only about what the container *could* hold, not how much it *does* hold. If you have a 4-ounce bottle that's half full, they'll still confiscate it. And why 3.4 ounces? Is there a difference between the explosions produced by a 3.4- and 3.5-ounce bottle of chemicals?

Well, anyway.

If you're a frequent traveler, you'll discover something peculiar about *toothpaste*. You might think that the best-selling tube size would be 3.1 ounces—logical enough, right?

But in fact, if you spend way too much time in the oral hygiene aisle of your drugstore, you'll find toothpaste packaged in these sizes: 0.8 ounces, 3.6 ounces, 4.0 ounces, 4.1 ounces, 4.2 ounces, 6.0 ounces, 6.2 ounces, 6.4 ounces, and 6.5 ounces. See anything missing in that list? Anyone? Anyone?

That's right: You can't *buy* a 3.4-ounce toothpaste!

The toothpaste-industrial complex would much rather make you buy lots of small tubes, at a much higher price per ounce— or a big tube, which the TSA will throw away so that you have to buy a replacement when you land.

You can save yourself a lot of money, time, and waste, though, if you buy your toothpaste *online*. On Amazon.com, for example, you'll find toothpaste available in non-drugstore sizes like 2.8 ounces. That's still not ideal—3.4 ounces would be ideal!—but it's much closer.

---

## PreCheck: Getting through security the 2001 way

There are so many reasons to be frustrated by the TSA (the Transportation Security Administration) and the bureaucracy created after 9/11 to make air travel safer. But there's one thing the TSA is doing right, and that's TSA PreCheck.

These are special lanes at airport security reserved for people the TSA has checked out in advance and found not to be security risks. In these lanes, you *don't* have to take off your shoes, belt, or jacket. You *don't* have to pull out your laptop and toiletries bag. You *don't* have to put your arms up inside some

whole-body scanner as if you're getting mugged. Instead, it's like traveling before 9/11 ever happened.

A couple of years ago, PreCheck was just a pilot program. You were selected to participate at random, and you didn't get to use the PreCheck lane every time.

But these days, you can also *apply* to be in PreCheck by visiting one of the offices at 300 airports around the country. You get fingerprinted and pay $85; if you're a US citizen and not a criminal, you'll get your Known Traveler Number in a couple of weeks. In general, if you enter this number when you're booking a flight, you'll get to use the PreCheck lanes at any of 120 US airports.

The takeaway here: First, check your boarding pass for the word *PreCheck* every time you fly, to see if you've won the TSA

lottery. Second, know what that *means*: You can use the speed lane, you don't have to take off your shoes, belt, or coat, and you can leave your laptop in your bag.

------------------------------------------------------------

# How to find room for your carry-on

As you know if you've flown recently, there's rarely enough room in the overhead bins for everybody's luggage. Very often, you discover that all the bins are full, and you're told you'll have to check your carry-on bag.

But here's a little secret that flight attendants know: There is *always* room for one more bag.

Think about it: The passengers who board first find *empty* bins. They have no incentive to place their stuff up there efficiently. It doesn't occur to them that space may eventually become tight. And once it does, most people have a "that's not my problem" attitude.

That's why, by the time you come along, you may discover that somebody has taken up two or three feet of bin space with something flat: a coat, a shopping bag, or a garment bag. Or someone might have laid a backpack or briefcase horizontally instead of sitting it upright. People often put their rolling luggage up there the long, wide way, even if the bin is deep enough to accommodate it wheels first.

With a small amount of rearranging, you can fit your bag, too. You've probably never made the attempt, though, because it involves touching other people's stuff. And that, of course, involves a social awkwardness that you may not want to confront.

But it's worth the effort. The moment of interaction will be over in 15 seconds—and because you didn't have to check your bag, you'll be on your way 20 minutes sooner when you land.

The trick is to put your bag *under* the coat, shopping bag, or garment bag. Or *turn* that backpack upright to make room. Or *turn* the other guy's rolling bag 90 degrees, wheels in. With only a few seconds of study, you can *always* find a little more space.

*Before*

*After*

If you have to move someone's clothing or shopping bag, consider announcing your intention first. Ask the passengers in that row: "Do you guys mind if I put my bag under this jacket up here?" Nobody ever minds. In fact, they'll wish they were as assertive and clever as you are.

---

# The noise-canceling earbuds that cost 28 cents

Hours of exposure to very loud engines—even inside the plane—is bad for your hearing *and* bad for your brain. It's fatiguing. If you can block out that noise, you land more refreshed.

For this reason, companies such as Bose have made a fortune selling noise-canceling headphones, at $300 a pair, to well-heeled frequent flyers. But you can achieve exactly the same effect for 28 cents—with foam earplugs from the drugstore.

If you haven't tried them in years, you'll be impressed at how far earplugs have come in comfort and noise-blocking ability. You squish them, slip them into your ears, and hold them in place for about 15 seconds. They slowly expand until they perfectly and comfortably block your ear canal, along with most of the decibels that are trying to get in. If your goal is noise cancellation, they are every bit as effective as headphones—but they don't need batteries, they take up no space at all in your carry-on, and, of course, they cost $299.72 less.

The sole disadvantage: You can't also listen to music or movies, as you can with noise-canceling headphones. But if your activities on the plane are sleeping or reading instead, these colorful little bits of foam might be the best in-flight upgrade you've ever received.

---

# The airplane pillow nobody knows

Some people can sleep on planes; some can't. Some people bring inflatable squishy neck rings to hold their heads up while they doze; some don't.

And some realize that an airplane's headrest has secret pillow flaps, and others don't.

On most modern airplanes, the headrest has flaps on either side of your head that you can grab with your hand and tug into position—as a support for both sides of your head.

There's a strong hinge inside, so each flap stays at the angle you choose. It's strong enough to stop your head from flopping onto your shoulder when you fall asleep. It's not *exactly* like a pillow, but it may add just enough support to help you drift off in flight.

---

# The armrest: One tip and one law

You do know that the armrest is hinged on most planes, right? It swings up and out of the way. That's exceptionally useful when there's an empty seat next to you and you want to

stretch out, or when you have a sleeping child, or when you want to snuggle with the person next to you (preferably somebody you know).

That's also exceptionally handy to remember in the *opposite* situation: When you arrive on the plane and find that there's *nothing* separating your flesh from the next passenger's. Chances are 100 percent that the armrest is there—it's just been swung upward.

And by the way: There should never be a fight over who gets the armrest. *The middle-seat passenger gets them both.* That's the great unwritten rule. Consider how miserable that person is, and yield one of your armrests.

# How to read fluently in other languages instantly

There's an app for that.

When you find yourself in a country where all the signs, maps, instructions, and menus are written in another language, fear not. Thanks to clever smartphone apps, you can read German, Spanish, French, Italian, Japanese, Chinese, and any of 85 other languages without a single lesson.

Install Google's free Google Translate app on your iPhone or Android phone. Now you can enter something to translate in any of four ways:

- **Type it.**

- **Write it with your finger** (great if you're standing in front of some sign where you don't even know what the *letters* are, such as Arabic or Japanese).

- Speak it.
- Take a picture of it with your phone's camera.

Instantly, Google Translate translates it into your language. It's the closest thing to a miracle you'll see in a long time.

As a handy bonus, at your option you can download the dictionaries to your phone so that no Internet connection is required. That's handy when you're in another country where you'd be charged $700 per word for a data connection.

---

# Spot your luggage at first sight

If you attach something bright and colorful to your bag, you'll identify it much faster when you have to grab it at the baggage claim. You'll also be far less likely to walk away with somebody else's luggage by accident.

It doesn't take an Einstein to think up this tip. It's easy, it's simple, and it works incredibly well.

Then how come so few people do it?

Go get a piece of ribbon, yarn, or colored tape, and put it on your bag *right now*. You'll be glad.

# Airline missed-flight policies: The Basics

If you fly much at all, sooner or later, something will go wrong. You'll miss the flight, or the flight will be delayed, or it will cancel the flight out from under you. What are your rights?

They're good to know. These, in general, are the policies of US airlines flying domestically.

- **If you miss your flight.** They'll try to book you on the same airline's next flight, usually at no charge. (Some airlines do charge a fee; for example, American charges $75.)

- **If you have to change your flight.** If you bought a nonrefundable ticket, you'll pay a $200 change fee to book a different flight. You may also pay more or less for the new ticket.

- **If your flight is delayed more than 4 hours.** If it's not the airline's fault—bad weather, for example—they'll try to rebook you on a later flight, same airline.

  If it *is* the airline's fault (mechanical problems, for example), they'll do more. They may try to book you on *another* airline, give you a hotel voucher, or give you a refund.

- **If you don't use your return ticket.** Nothing. You don't get your money back, but there are no other repercussions.

- **If your flight is delayed and you miss your connection.** They'll book you on another flight, even on a different airline if necessary.

- **If you're flying to a funeral.** Last-minute fares are always the most expensive ones. So airlines used to offer *bereavement fares*—lower prices for people who have to travel for the death, or imminent death, of an immediate family member.

  Most airlines have eliminated this kindness in the past couple of years. (Delta still offers special fares, or fares with travel-date flexibility; if you're on the road and need to get home quickly, Delta will also waive the change fee for your return flight. You may have to supply the address of the hospital or funeral home.)

# Cheaper hotel prices on your phone

If you need a last-minute hotel room—a few days in advance, or even same-day—you'll save a lot of money if you book it using your smartphone. (Use an app like Hipmunk or Hotel Tonight, or even your phone's Web browser.) If you book the room on your computer, you'll pay much higher prices.

*Computer*                    *Phone*

The reason: Hotels are desperate to avoid having empty, unrented rooms. They'd rather earn *something* for one of those rooms than nothing at all. So they post deeply discounted rates to phone apps and phone Web browsers in hopes of reaching the kind of mobile, spontaneous people who could fill up those otherwise unrented rooms. —*Adam Goldstein*

# The dewrinkling chamber in every hotel

If your dressy shirt, jacket or dress got wrinkled in your luggage, all is not lost. In any hotel room more expensive than about $25 a night, there's an iron and ironing board in the closet.

Is the wrinkly thing not something you can iron? Then hang it on the shower rod in the bathroom, turn on the shower at its hottest setting, leave the bathroom, and close the door. (Contrary to gut instinct, this trick doesn't work if you're *in* the shower; to produce the necessary steam, the water has to be hotter than you'd like it.)

After ten minutes, the steam and humidity relax the fibers of your clothing, letting the wrinkles fall away. Turn off the water, let the steam air out, and let the clothing cool before putting it on.

# How to close your hotel-room curtains

Why would you book a hotel room? Well, one plausible reason is that you might want a place to *sleep*.

But between the noises in the hallway, the deafening air conditioning, the unfamiliarity of the bed, and the light let in by the curtains that never close all the way, there's a pretty good chance you won't sleep as well as you do at home.

You can, fortunately, fight back.

For example, you *can* make the curtains close. Sometimes they leave a gap, and sometimes they're being blown open by the air conditioner. Either way, the sunlight will start blasting you awake at 5:45 A.M.

Here are three ways to pin the curtains closed before you turn out the light.

- **Pull them so that they overlap,** and then lean the desk chair against them, pinning them against the window.

- **Grab a pen from the desk,** and use its pocket clip to pin the curtains together at the bottom edge.

- **For a more professional tool,** travel with a binder clip (one of those big black metal spring-loaded paper clips). Use it to pin the curtains closed.

The hard part may be remembering to *do* this when you go to bed. At night, it might not occur to you to imagine how bright the curtain gap will be at the crack of dawn.

---

# How to fold a jacket so it doesn't get crumpled in your bag

This one's a terrific old tailor trick. It's a way to fold a blazer or suit jacket so that you can pack it into an overnight bag, carry-on bag, or rolling bag—without getting it rumpled or wrinkled.

1. **Face the jacket** as though you're going to put it on backward. Insert your hands into the shoulder holes, so that the jacket hangs that way.

2. **Bring your palms** (and the jacket shoulders) together, as shown in Figure A.

3. **Grab the collar** that's now above your left wrist (B). Pull it forward and around to the right, rotating your left wrist so that the left jacket shoulder turns *inside out* around the other shoulder (C). Withdraw your hands and grab the collar so that the jacket is hanging nicely. Give the whole thing a shake.

4. **Slip the whole thing** into a plastic bag, of the type that dry cleaners put on a newly cleaned shirt or coat. The slipperiness of the bag keeps your coat from bunching up against other things in your luggage and then wrinkling.

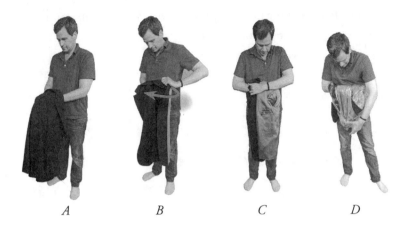

|  |  |  |  |
|---|---|---|---|
| *A* | *B* | *C* | *D* |

5. **Fold the jacket in half** to fit into your bag (D). If the suitcase has straps, use them to pin the bundle down, so it won't move in transit.

As soon as you get to your destination, pull the jacket out of the bag, unfold it, and hang it up. (Keep the plastic bag; you'll need it again when you travel home.) Nobody will ever suspect that it crossed the country wedged into luggage half its size.

------------------------------------------------

# Surviving Disney World

Show me a parent with young children, and I'll show you an adult brain quivering with guilt and fear about Disney World. A visit there is an unforgettable experience for a kid, of course. But it's also a trip to a crowded, expensive tourist trap where you'll spend hours standing in lines for rides that are over in 90 seconds.

If you're willing to make an expensive trip even more expensive, you can buy a Fast Pass. That's a golden ticket that gives you an appointment to ride a certain ride at a certain time. At that point, you can skip the line.

You can also use the free alternative: the Disney World *app.* This incredible software reveals, on your smartphone, how long the line is at every ride in the park, in real time. As your young Disneyphiles pour off of one ride, you can consult the app to see which next stop has the shortest wait.

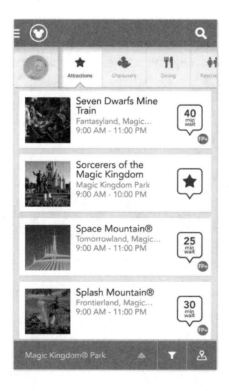

# How to fight the tyranny of the duvet

Aduvet ("doo-VAY") is a big, thick, fluffy quilt. It's soft. It's usually white. It's supposed to be luxurious and trendy.

It's taking over hotel rooms worldwide. In the old days, your hotel bed was made of layers: a sheet, then a blanket or two, and then a bedspread.

Today? A duvet.

Apparently, the hotel industry never got the memo: A duvet may be big, thick, fluffy, and white, but it's an all-or-nothing. You can't peel back a layer of it when you get hot. You either boil or you freeze.

If you prefer something not quite as suffocating on top of you all night, what are you supposed to do?

Get clever, that's what. Upon inspection, you'll discover that the duvet has a *cover,* much the way a pillow has a pillowcase. What you've got is a thick quilt inside a huge cloth bag.

If you pull the quilt out of its cloth envelope, you're left with just the cover—something like the world's thinnest, softest sleeping bag. Throw the quilt on the floor, and use the cover as your blanket. Presto: You've got yourself what feels like a couple of sheets on top of you, and you'll no longer burn to a crackly crisp from your own body heat.

---

# Jet lag: The Basics

Jet lag is the grogginess, sleeplessness, and sometimes stomach problems that strike you when you fly to a distant time zone (from the US to Europe or Asia, for example). The sunlight and eating patterns of the new locale throw off your body's circadian rhythms. For example, your eyes see the sun high in the sky, but your brain, stuck on your home schedule, still believes it to be the middle of the night.

To feel fully yourself again, it usually takes one day for each couple of time zones you've crossed; longer if you're older.

Over the years, travelers, doctors, and lunatics have proposed all kinds of purported cures for jet lag. Things to eat, things to drink, small animals to sacrifice.

But if you'd like to know what *really* works, here's what research studies suggest:

- **Shift in advance.** If you're flying eastward: Start going to bed earlier and eating meals earlier. If you're flying west: Start staying up and eating meals later. The idea is to simulate the new time zone before you get there.

Similarly, experts suggest that you set your watch to the new time zone on the plane—a psychological fake-out.

Finally, if it's daytime where you're going, try to stay awake on the plane. If it's nighttime where you're going, try to sleep. (Lots of people take melatonin pills for this purpose—take them an hour before your *new* bedtime, and prepare to be groggy for eight hours—but the studies on its ability to minimize jet lag are so far inconclusive.)

- **Drink on the flight.** Part of the problem, experts say, is the way plane travel dehydrates you. There's about 12 percent humidity in an aircraft cabin—drier than a desert. Drink a lot during the flight (but not alcohol, which will dehydrate you further).

- **Let the sun help you.** Once you've landed, spend some time in the sun: in the afternoon if you flew to the east, in the morning if you flew to the west. That sunlight exposure helps shift your body's internal clock to the new time zone.

- **Take a hot bath.** When you're at your destination, a hot bath at bedtime can help you fall asleep at the new bedtime—because it's relaxing and because your body temperature drops as you get *out* of the tub, which can make you sleepy.

- **Diets don't matter.** Research shows that no particular kinds of foods affect jet lag.

# Chapter 3: **Food**

There are as many essentials to learn about food as there are different kinds of it. How do you choose it? How do you know if it's ripe? How do you cook it? How do you serve it?

And how do you get ketchup out of the bottle?

On the following pages: a sampling of the finest info bits.

---

## The ancient Incan ritual for extracting ketchup

According to tribal lore (as well as the Heinz Web site), there's a special significance to the number *57* that's molded into the glass Heinz ketchup bottle: You can bang that exact spot with the heel of your palm a few times to get the ketchup flowing.

(Why, with more than 5,500 products, does Heinz still use 57 as its marketing number? Because founder Henry Heinz used to

*Bang here.*

advertise his "57 varieties" back in 1896. Even though, back then, the company was already selling *60* different products. Mr. Heinz thought 57 was catchier.)

## The scientific method for extracting ketchup

N ot all ketchup comes from Heinz, and not all ketchup comes in tall glass bottles. So how are you supposed to get the ketchup out of *other* containers? Especially when there's only a little bit left at the bottom?

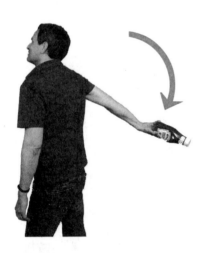

Use centrifugal force. Hold the bottle at the bottom. Make sure the lid is on securely. Swing your arm in a big circle a couple of times. You'll discover that (a) the ketchup is forced to the top of the bottle, ready for dispensing, and (b) the other people at the barbecue look at you funny.

Special note for those with rotator-cuff injuries: If you find it difficult or painful to swing the ketchup bottle over your head— well, do you want that condiment or don't you, wimp?

No, just kidding. There's an alternate centrifugal-force method that can also help you: Holding the bottle upside-down over your burger, swirl your hand around in little circles. Try to make a very tiny, very slow tomato tornado against the sides of the bottle. After a moment, the ketchuppy lava will flow.

# Expand-O ketchup cups

Many a fast-food restaurant or cafeteria offers small white paper cups, which you're supposed to fill with ketchup or mustard from the dispensers before heading to your table.

Upon closer inspection, you'll discover two facts about these cups:

- **They're made of white paper,** folded up accordion style for added structural strength.

- **They don't hold very much.**

Those are, in fact, two *related* facts. Because if you tug on the paper cup's rim, unfolding the pleats, you wind up making the cup bigger, so it holds more.

Anyone at your table who intends to help themselves to your fries will be appreciative.

# A life-changing tip for people who buy natural peanut butter

Brand-name regular peanut butter—Jif, Peter Pan, Skippy, and so on—has a lot more in it than peanuts. You're also getting sugar, oil, mono- and diglycerides, and so on.

*Natural* peanut butter is nothing but peanuts and maybe salt. Some people consider it tastier and healthier. Some people also consider it a real pain to use, because when you open the jar, there's a pool of peanut oil sitting on top of the butter. It's your job to stir the oil back into the peanut sludge before eating, which is tricky and messy.

But not if you store the jar upside down! In that case, the oil rises to the *bottom* of the jar. You'll be able to stir it much more easily and efficiently—without any oil mess at all.

# Leave the butter out

Cold, hard butter from the fridge is really hard to spread on bread. You wind up tearing the bread and depositing the butter unevenly. Life's rough, right?

Anyway, the solution is ridiculously easy: Leave your butter *out* of the fridge. Leave it on the counter, where it's easy to grab—and soft—whenever you have to spread it onto something.

You're probably thinking, "No way! It's a dairy product! It'll spoil!"

Actually not. Bacteria need moisture to flourish—and butter is made almost completely of fat. It began life as cream; furthermore, that cream's been pasteurized, killing all sick-making bacteria. Finally, the salt in most butter makes it even more unlikely for bacteria to gain a foothold.

Bottom line: You won't get sick from butter you've left out for a few weeks.

You may, however, discover that it eventually *tastes* funny if it's exposed to light and oxygen. Therefore, keep it in a covered, opaque butter dish.

This simple change will bring tremendous happiness to your life.

On the other hand, you'll find yourself using *more* butter this way.

So, you know—even more happiness.

# How to rinse fresh mushrooms

You rinse mushrooms in water, of course.

If you're a longtime cook, that simple statement might be causing your palms to sweat and pupils to dilate. For decades, conventional wisdom has told us that mushrooms are like sponges—that if you put them in water, they'll soak up moisture and won't cook properly.

"Use a damp paper towel or a soft mushroom brush to wipe each mushroom, one at a time," says the Better Homes & Gardens Web site to this day. "Do not soak the mushrooms. Because they absorb water like little sponges, mushrooms won't brown nicely when cooked if they are full of water."

But it's not true.

*The New York Times*, *The Guardian*, TV's Alton Brown, and many individual chefs have all done comparison tests, rinsing half the mushrooms and hand-rubbing the other half (with a "soft mushroom brush," no doubt). After cooking, the mushrooms look and taste identical.

So rinse away, cooks of the world. You'll be able to get dinner on that much sooner.

# The Great Garlic Husk Trick

Garlic, as you probably know, comes prepackaged by Nature with a convenient wrapper: its skin, its husk. Convenient, that is, until you want to remove it.

Why not let Nature remove it for you, too?

Put the garlic in a hard, enclosed container—a pot with a lid, for example, or two metal bowls placed mouth to mouth. Shake hard, for maybe 15 seconds.

When you stop, you'll find that the garlic is now naked and shivering, its wrapper in shreds nearby.

---

# Flatten your meat

Experienced family food providers divide their ground beef into individual ziplock bags before freezing it. These individual meat packs will be much easier to thaw and prepare when the time comes. (The same principle applies to tomato sauce, cookie dough, stew, and so on.)

*Really* experienced family food providers *flatten* the meat before freezing it. Flatter packages are faster to freeze, easier to stack, and faster to thaw.

# The better way
# to peel a banana

Most people attempt to open a banana's peel using the stem as a pull tab. Sometimes that works. But often, especially if the banana is a little green, that process winds up mushing the banana top into baby food. You also wind up having to pick away the stringy bits.

You'll avoid both problems if you open the banana from the *other* end.

(Most people think of a banana's opposite end as its "bottom." But in fact, bananas grow in bunches *upward* from the stem—so technically, the "bottom" is the top. There. Now you won't embarrass yourself at a Chiquita company picnic.)

Pinch the black crusty end point, splitting it. Now you can tug the peels away.

*Start here*

This method is better than the stem-opening tradition in three ways:

- **You avoid mushing** or bruising the first bite.

- **No stringy parts!** (They peel away with the peel.)

- **The stem acts** as a handy handling handle when you've eaten your way to the bottom.

(On the Internet, you can read that this is how monkeys eat bananas— aren't they smart? But in fact, monkeys open their bananas from the bottom, from the top, or from the side—whichever seems easiest at the time. Apparently, they don't get on the Internet much.)

------------------------------------------------

# Chopping an onion: The Basics

As everybody knows, cutting an onion releases a sulfuric chemical called syn-propanethial-S-oxide. It rises to your face as a gas, and then next thing you know, your eyes are watering—your body's desperate attempt to flush the acid out. That's why you cry when you cut an onion.

On the Internet, there's a "how to avoid onion crying" tip for every man, woman, and child: chewing bread while you cut, chewing gum, keeping a spoon in your mouth, breathing only through your nose, and so on.

But the science says that these are the ones that work:

- **Use a sharp knife.** The sharper the knife, the fewer onion cells you break open, and the less gas you release.

- **Chill the onion first.** Thirty minutes in the fridge, or 10 minutes in the freezer. Less syn-propanethial-S-oxide will evaporate.

- **Blow the gases away.** Turn on your stove's exhaust fan, set up a portable fan, or even blow gently at the onion as you cut it.

- **Cut under a thin stream of water on a cutting board.** The water keeps the gases from rising to your face.

- Cut as closely (and as safely) as you can to a candle. Somehow the flame interferes with the sulfur gas molecules reaching your face.

The most effective method of all: Wear swim goggles. That practice, however, guarantees quizzical looks from the kitchen passersby.

---

# The axle you didn't know your plastic wrap had

There's a secret feature lurking on the ends of your plastic wrap's cardboard box: little triangular cardboard tabs. You're supposed to pop them inward.

You've now made, in effect, an axle that holds the roll of plastic wrap in place as you unroll it!

# Where to find cooler food in your bowl

What do you do when the food in your bowl—soup, chili, oatmeal, mac and cheese—is still too hot from cooking? Most people have only one tactic: blowing on each mouthful.

There is, however, another technique at your disposal: Take small bites from around the edges of the bowl. The food there is always a few degrees cooler than what's in the center. The bowl is shallower there, and the bowl itself has cooled the hot stuff down where it touches.

# The ultimate guide to knowing about an egg

You want to know the problem with eggs? They have shells. You can't see inside them. How do you know if an egg is rotten? Or hard-boiled? The wise lifers on Twitter know:

- **Twirl the egg on your countertop.** If it spins, it's hard-boiled. If not, it's raw. (The contents of the uncooked egg are runny, so they slosh around, resisting the spin. The cooked egg's center of gravity, on the other hand, doesn't change.) —*Barb Hagerman*

- **Put a questionable egg into a bowl of water.** If it sinks, it's OK to eat, even if it's past the due date written on the carton. If it's rotten, it floats, thanks to the gas that has accumulated inside. (Iffy ones touch the bottom, standing on end.) —*Jay Lyerly*

---

# The ultimate guide to cooking with eggs

You want to know the great thing about eggs? They have shells. That's built-in protection.

There's a trick, however, to getting the eggy stuff *out* of the shelly stuff:

- Instead of cracking an egg on the *edge* of the pan, bowl, or counter, crack it on a flat surface. That way, the shell cracks without the yoke spilling out or shell fragments falling into your breakfast-to-be. —*Stephen Campbell*

- Once you've boiled an egg, you have to get the shell off of it. Here's the easiest way.

- First, crack the shell around the equator (middle ring) of the egg. Roll it around on the counter to make the cracks even finer.

- Next, peel away the cracked shells from the equator, leaving a bare strip around the middle. At this point, you can pop the top and bottom halves of the shell off.

(By the way: The shell is even easier to peel if you've put the egg in cold water for a few minutes after cooking, so that the shell and membrane separate a bit.) —*Leon Wong*

---

# How to remember how to set the utensils

When you're setting the table, you probably know that you're supposed to put the knife, fork, and spoon on both sides of the plate. But if this isn't the sort of thing you do every day, how are you supposed to remember *where* they go? Which ones go on the left side and which on the right?

- The *order* of silverware is easy to remember: It's alphabetical! **F**ork, **K**nife, **S**poon.

- The **side of the plate** is easy to remember, too: The word fork has the same number of letters as left. The words knife and spoon each have the same number of letters as right.

Right? —*Robert Rudin*

# The right way to pour from a box of liquid

W hen you pour liquid from a can," your mom probably told you, "use the can opener to make holes on both sides of the lid. That way, the air can come in one hole, while the liquid pours out the other."

Well, guess what? The same principle applies when you're pouring from one of those rectangular, waxed-cardboard boxes of liquid: broth, soup, almond milk, chai tea, and so on.

You'll be able to pour much more steadily, with more control and better speed, if you poke an airhole into the top of the carton, on the side opposite that of the pouring spout.

------------------------------------------------------------

# How to quench a spicy mouth on fire

When you take a bite that's much spicier than you expected, it's no fun. It's *pain*. Your mouth is on fire, and you want to put it out *now*.

Unfortunately, most people's instinct is to gulp water. That's how you put out a real fire, right?

With spice, though, that's the *worst* thing you can do. The burning sensation in spicy food is caused by an oil from the hot peppers called capsaicin (cap-SAY-sin).

Oil and water don't mix. So if you drink water (or beer), you just wash that burning chemical into new places in your mouth. It's the same reason you can't put out a chemical fire with a fire hose—you're just pushing the chemicals around.

What *does* put out a capsaicin fire in your mouth? Fat, oil, alcohol, and "soak up" foods. For example:

- **Dairy products.** Whole milk. Yogurt. Butter. Sour cream. Ice cream. The milk proteins and fat bind with capsaicin oil and wash it away.

- **Oily products.** Peanut butter and olive oil are the oily ingredients you're most likely to have handy in a restaurant. Here again, the oil binds with the capsaicin and gets it off your taste buds.

- **Alcohol.** Yes, alcohol can also dissolve capsaicin. But we're talking high alcohol content (like vodka), not something that's mostly water (like beer).

- **Sponge foods.** Starches like white rice and bread can soak up the capsaicin oil, leaving less of it on your flesh to burn you.

Then, for best results, don't take another bite of whatever got you into trouble.

--------------------------------------------------------------

# How to stop apples from turning brown

Once you expose an apple's insides to the air, they begin *oxidizing*—an enzyme in the juice reacts with the oxygen in the air and turns the white part brown. It doesn't affect the taste much, but it's a visual turnoff, especially for discerning consumers under 12 years old.

Scientists are, in fact, working on developing new apple breeds that don't contain the culprit chemical and won't turn brown. Until they succeed, you have two options:

- **Keep the air away from the cut parts.** If you've cut an entire apple into slices, store it back in its original form, held together by a rubber band. Without exposure to the air, the apple flesh won't oxidize.

- **Use the old lemon-juice trick.** Citric acid is an antioxidant; it stops the browning in its tracks. Lemon juice, lime juice, orange juice, and pineapple juice all contain citric acid in abundance.

You can just pour or sprinkle the juice onto the cut apples—pineapple juice is usually a taste hit with the younger set. Or you can soak the slices in a bowl of anti-browning potion (a cup of water with a tablespoon of lemon or lime juice in it).

If you're hard-core, you can also buy a bottled citric-acid *powder* called Fruit-Fresh that's precisely for this problem.

All of these tricks work equally well with other fruit that oxidizes, like bananas, pears, peaches, and avocados.

--------------------------------------------------

# The universal kitchen timer

If you have a kitchen timer, great. If you have a timer app on your smartphone, great.

But if you have neither, go to Google.com. In the search box, type in "Set timer for 5 min" (or whatever timing you need). When you click Start, you get a countdown. (If you click the ⌐ ⌐ icon, the timer fills your entire screen, for visibility from across the room—or across town.)

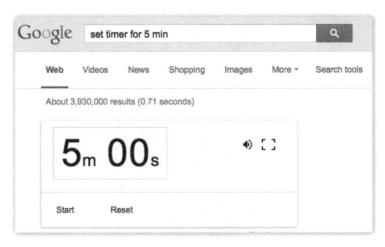

Google   set timer for 5 min   🔍

**Web**   Videos   News   Shopping   Images   More ▾   Search tools

About 3,930,000 results (0.71 seconds)

## 5ₘ 00ₛ   ◀) ⌐ ⌐

Start    Reset

When the timer reaches zero, your computer/phone/tablet thing plays a sound (unless you've clicked the ◀)) icon to mute it).

Great for board games and family arguments, too!

---

# Opening a jar: The Basics

I f you can't seem to unscrew a super tight jar lid bare-handed, use one of these tricks. They work every time:

- **Put a fat rubber band** around the rim of the lid. Now you've got the grip of Superman, and the force of your turning is magnified greatly.

- **Wedge a spoon under** the edge of the lid. Use it like a lever to pull the metal out slightly. As in the previous trick, the idea is to break the vacuum seal. Once the seal pops, the lid unscrews easily!

- **Confidently rap the lid's edge** against the floor. If you do it hard enough, you'll make a nearly imperceptible *dent* in the metal, which lets in air, which breaks the vacuum seal, which makes the lid unscrew easily.

-------------------------------------------------------------

# How to stop the pot from boiling over

You know all those goofy "life hacks" that people send around on the Internet? Well, *one* of them is worth learning—it's quick, easy, and it really works.

A pot of water doesn't boil over if you lay a wooden spoon across the top of the pot.

Why does it work? Two reasons. First, the dry wood itself pops the tiny bubbles of the foam.

Second, the spoon is a lot *cooler* than the steam inside the bubbles. When the bubble hits the wood, the steam condenses back into water, and the bubble bursts.

That's why you can't use a *metal* spoon; it heats up rapidly and loses the temperature differential.

You also shouldn't use a *plastic* spoon. When it melts into the pot, it makes your food taste funny.

------------------------------------------------------------

# The painfully simple trick for scooping out hard ice cream

Ready?

Run your spoon under hot water first. That's it.

You'll find that the spoon cuts through the hard ice cream as though it's...*soft* ice cream.

If you're *eating* hard ice cream, you may prefer to keep a *mug* of hot water next to you, so you can dip your spoon into it after each delicious, melty mouthful.

------------------------------------------------------------

# The quick way to clean a blender

After you've used your blender to whip up some delicious smoothies, pancake batter, hummus, pesto, salsa, guacamole, salad dressing, or tapenade, you're left with the less delicious task of *cleaning* that blender.

Well, if spinning deadly blades made the mess, they can clean it up, too.

Fill the blender halfway with water…add a drop of dish soap…and run it.

Then rinse with hot water. Presto: clean blender.

---

# The Great Jelly-Spreading Lie

The world wants you to believe that a knife is the best implement for spreading jelly, butter, and cream cheese onto bread. It's not.

The spoon is a better choice. Specifically, the back of it.

First, its larger surface area distributes the spreading pressure, so it's less likely to tear the bread. Second, when you need to scoop into the container for more jelly or cream cheese—well, it's a spoon.

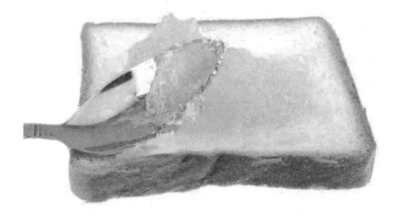

# Instant counter space

Every now and then, you'll encounter a situation when you'll wish you had more counter space. Thanksgiving for 20 people, for example. Or an apartment in New York.

That's the beauty of drawers and cutting boards. Pull out a drawer, lay a cutting board across it, and boom: instant counter space.

You can probably figure out how to reverse the procedure on your own.

# Lazy Susan in the fridge

In moments of intense boredom, you may realize how goofy it is that a refrigerator—the box in your house that you open the *most frequently*—is opaque and solid on three sides. That quirk explains the Fridge Shelf Shuffle: the time-consuming, energy-wasting moments of foraging that you must occasionally undertake when you're trying to find what you want.

A lazy Susan—one of those rotating platters—is the simple solution. Why aren't they built into refrigerators in the first place?

# Rescue bread from the brink of death

From the moment it comes out of the baker's oven, bread begins losing moisture. If a loaf of *your* bread is entering the kingdom of staleness, you can get at least another good day out of it with this bread-zombie trick:

Put the loaf under running water. Seriously. Get the crust really wet.

Set the bread into your oven, right on the rack, and heat at 300 degrees for 6 to 12 minutes, depending on the size of the loaf and how wet it is.

Amazingly, the steam makes the inside soft and moist, and the oven makes the crust firm and crackly. You're ready to sandwichify.

# Rescue greens from the brink of death

Greens—lettuce, kale, cabbage, chard, what have you—wilt over time. They turn dark and slimy. No news there.

*Wilted*

*Revived!*

But it's not because they're rotting; it's because they're *dehydrating*.

You can reanimate them by soaking them in lukewarm water for half an hour or so. Then rinse them with cold water, and marvel at their restored crispness and attractiveness.

------------------------------------------------

## Can of soda: straw holder

This is an old Internet classic, but it's handy:

Use the pop-top of a can of soda to stop the straw from popping up out of the drink.

------------------------------------------------

## How to light a bunch of candles with a single match

Simple: Use a stick of uncooked spaghetti. It works like a very long match and burns with an even, long-lasting flame.

It gives you plenty of time to move from candle to candle, lighting them all with that one noodle.

The spaghetti-match trick is also worth remembering when you have to light a pilot burner way inside some grill, fireplace, oven, or stove, or you're trying to light a candle whose wick is way down at the bottom of a container. It's like a footlong match.

# How to store cucumbers so they don't get gross

If you don't refrigerate a cucumber, it will get soft and disgusting within 48 hours.

If you just put the cucumber into the fridge naked (the cuke, not you), it will get soft and wrinkly, and lose its crispness and flavor.

If you put the cucumber into a plastic *bag* in the fridge, it will get slimy in a few days (the cucumber, not the bag).

The secret: Wrap the cucumber in a paper towel and put *that* into a plastic bag in the fridge. The cucumber will look, feel, and taste perfect even after a week.

Incredibly, the paper towel trick works even on the *cut end* of a cucumber. That end won't get slimy or soft, either, if it's pressed against a paper towel. It's a miracle of modern science.

(The paper towel trick also works on cut lettuce. You can even lay one across the top of one of those clear-plastic containers of grocery-store, ready-to-eat salad mixes to keep it from getting slimy.)

--------------------------------------------------------

# Restore crystallized honey

First of all, crystals forming in your bottle of honey doesn't mean it's gone bad; it's not like a battery or something. Crystallization is normal—so normal that honey crystallizes *in the beehive* if the weather gets chilly.

The crystals represent the separation of the two kinds of sugar that make up honey: glucose and fructose. The speed of crystallization depends on the container (glass bottles = slower crystallizing), the temperature of the cabinet (cooler temperatures speed up crystals), and whether the honey has been filtered (which reduces the likelihood of crystallization).

In any case, putting it all back together again is as simple as heating the honey. You can do that either in the microwave (try 15 seconds for the first round) or by putting the honey bottle into hot water for a few minutes.

Once the honey cools, though, it will recrystallize. And after several cycles of heating/cooling, the honey will start to lose its flavor and scent. So the best technique is to heat only as much as you need—or to learn to like crystallized honey.

Yes, some people *prefer* their honey crystallized; it tastes good, and it doesn't drip. Worldwide, in fact, more people buy factory-crystallized honey (in forms called creamed, spun, whipped, or churned) than runny honey.

---

## Buy these containers and praise the gods of science

In general, this book tiptoes very carefully to avoid telling you what to *buy*. It's a book of wisdom, not endorsements.

But these, you should buy. Your life will change profoundly.

They're glass bowls with airtight lids; you get various sizes in a set. You can microwave in these bowls, serve in them, freeze in them—and, above all, store the leftovers in them. In other words, after a meal, you have *one* bowl to wash instead of three or four.

The leftovers thing is the best. You don't have to use any landfill-clogging plastic wrap, since the lids are airtight—and you can *see* what's in these bowls as they sit on your fridge shelf. They stack beautifully in there, too.

There are many brands: Anchor, Pyrex, Snaplock, Kinetic, Rubbermaid. All of them can go from freezer to oven to table to dishwasher in one dish.

Every cook should be issued a set of these bowls.

# Chapter 4: **Clothes**

It's an almost ironclad rule: Sooner or later, you're going to have to wear clothes.

Considering how much time you're going to spend in them and around them, you may as well master their darkest secrets.

-------------------------------------------------------------

## The right way to tie your shoes

Maybe you know a kid. Maybe *you* were once a kid. Either way, you know about the tendency of shoelaces to come untied.

The reason is very simple: You've been tying your shoes wrong your whole life.

To use the technical term, you've been tying granny knots. You can tell because the loops of the bow have a tendency to run heel to toe, rather than lying nicely horizontally.

By making a simple change in the usual bow-tying sequence, you can produce the correct, sturdy bowknot instead of the granny—and the shoes won't come untied.

You know the first step of tying your shoes, the part where you tuck one lace under the other and pull tight (Figure 1)?

*Figure 1*

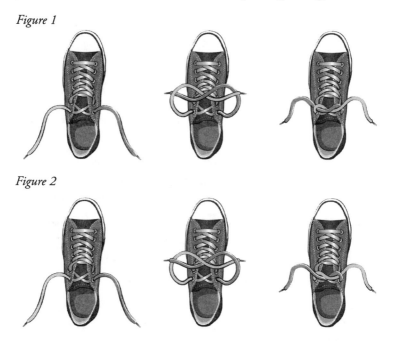

*Figure 2*

The trick is to *reverse* the laces. Instead of wrapping the left end over the right, wrap the right end over the left (Figure 2). When you complete the bowmaking business and pull tight, the loops lie horizontally across the shoe—and the knot won't come undone!

--------------------------------------------------------

## The right way to untie your shoes

When you want to undo shoelaces you've tied in the standard bow, it's annoying, isn't it, when you grab the *wrong* end? You pull it and wind up making only a tighter knot?

That won't happen anymore. Because now you know that you should always grab the *shorter* loose end. When you tug *that* one, the knot always dissolves.

---

# The mystery of the extra shoelace hole

They've been there for years, mystifying anyone who bothered to ponder them: an extra set of shoelace holes on running shoes, right near the ankle. They're slightly out of alignment with the regular holes—so what are they for?

They're for a *heel lock*. That's a special lace-tying technique that does a better job of securing the fabric of the shoe around your ankle—and minimizes the chance that your heel will slosh around while hiking (causing blisters) or that you'll bang against the front of the shoe while distance running (causing black-toenail syndrome—don't ask).

You create a heel lock (sometimes called a lace lock) *before* tying your shoe. First, run the lace that's hanging off the right side through the top heel-lock hole of the same side, creating a loop; do the same on the left side.

Next, cross each lace end through the loop you've just made on the opposite side, as shown by the arrow below.

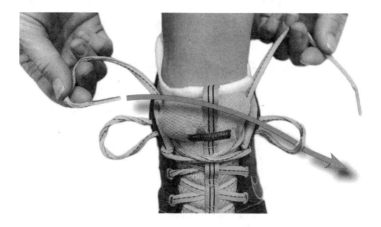

Cinch tight (pull down, not up) so that the shoe hugs the top of your foot.

Now tie your shoes as usual.

You'll enjoy a much snugger fit—and the satisfaction of knowing, at last, why there are two extra holes in your shoes!

# How to prevent your flip-flop plug from popping out

Yes, yes, OK, your flip-flops cost only $6, and they're made of foam rubber from China. But it's still a pain when you pull the toe-pole out of the little hole in the sole, sometimes ruining your footwear for good.

If you'd like to stave off that disaster, protect the plug with one of those plastic closing tabs from a bread wrapper—or cut out a disk from a margarine-tub lid. Either way, you've now got a hedge against flip-flop-plug pull-through.

# Three things to do with a new men's suit jacket

Cut off the little white tags on the sleeves.

Cut open the sewn-shut pockets. (They're not supposed to *stay* shut.)

Pull off the white basting thread on the shoulders and vents.

# Men's clothing: The Basics

Here, guys. This tidy list spares you 10 years of reading *GQ* and *Esquire* to glean the essentials of what's considered modern style.

- Your shoes and belt should match: brown with brown, or black with black.

- No matter how many buttons your jacket has, don't button the bottom one.

- Don't wear suspenders *and* a belt; one at a time.

- Your pants should be long enough to touch and "break" (bend) slightly at the tops of your shoes.

- Your sleeve should show about a half inch of shirt at your wrist.

- When it's tied right, the tip of the tie should touch the top of your belt.

- When wearing shorts, no socks (at least no visible ones).

- No socks with sandals.

- The socks should match the pants.

- White socks: for athletics only.

- If you tuck in your shirt, wear a belt.

Of course, the essence of style is being who you are; nobody should be able to tell you how to dress!

On the other hand: Before you become a rule-breaker, it's often helpful to know what the rules *are*.

------------------------------------------------

# The Great American Dictionary of Dress-Code Shorthand

There it is, on your invitation to something: "Business casual." Or "Smart casual." Or "Active attire." Or "Informal." What are they supposed to mean, and what's the ranking of formality? You don't want to be the only one at the boss's retirement party wearing shorts, right?

Here's a hugely simplified cheat sheet.

- **White tie.** Men: black dress coat or tailcoat, white vest, white bow tie. Women: floor-length evening gown.

- **Black tie.** Men: tuxedo, black vest or cummerbund. (If it says "Black tie optional," then a dark suit and tie are OK, too.) Women: long evening gown or dressy cocktail dress.

- **Semiformal.** Men: dark business suit, tie. Women: cocktail dress; long, dressy skirt and top; or little black dress.

- **Festive attire.** Men: sport coat, open-collar shirt, slacks. Women: cocktail dress; long, dressy skirt and top; or dressy pants outfit.

- **Business formal.** Men: dark business suit, tie. Women: suit, business-style dress, or dress with jacket.

- **Cocktail attire/informal.** Men: dark suit. Women: short, elegant dress.

- **Business casual/smart casual.** Dozens of definitions are bubbling through the clothesosphere. But this much is clear: For men, it's slacks and a collared or a button-down shirt. (A blazer is sometimes mentioned.) For women, pants or knee-length skirt, and blouse or collared shirt. For both: no jeans, no shorts, no athletic wear.

- **Casual.** Anything. Jeans, T-shirt or polo shirt, sneakers—all fine.

-------------------------------------------------

# How to find that contact lens, tiny screw, or earring

Dropped it on the floor, did you? Don't do that *hilarious* thing they always do in movies, where the guy who dropped the object walks around, slowly peering across the floor, until his next step produces a sickening *crunch*.

Instead, use a rubber band to strap a piece of thin cloth or mesh over the end of a vacuum-cleaner nozzle. Use a piece of nylon stocking, for example, or a thin sock, cloth handkerchief, or T-shirt.

As you slowly vacuum the floor, the suction will eventually pluck up your contact lens, screw, or earring—and make it stick to the fabric.

---

# Laundry: The Basics

If you've been doing laundry for years, congratulations! But if you're just starting out in the washer/dryer room, here are the principles:

- Wash white and light-colored clothes separately from dark and colored clothes. That's to avoid the dye from the dark clothes running onto the light ones. (Red polo shirt + white underwear = pink undies.)

- Inspect each article before you put it into the machine. Check the pockets. If you see a stain, spray it, front and back, with a pretreating spray or gel like Resolve, Tide Boost, or Shout.

- In the days of yore (yore parents, for example), you were told to use warm water for whites/lights, and cold water for colored/dark clothing. These days, though, liquid laundry detergent is formulated to work in hot *or* cold water—so now you can use cold water for *all* your laundry. Yes, radical but true. Your clothing will last longer, and you'll save money, because your hot-water heater can take a break.

- Pour the detergent into the bottle cap, which serves as a measuring cup, and empty the detergent into the washing machine.

- When the washing cycle is complete, pull out each piece of clothing and shake it out before putting it into the dryer.

- The dryer is deadly for the four *s*'s: sexy, stretchy, see-through, or sweatery.

- Don't hang stretchy or sweatery to dry, either—it will stretch. Lay it flat to dry.

--------------------------------------------------------------

# How to choose the right eyeglass frames for your face

Maybe you'll find a pair of frames and fall in love with them. In that case, great.

But if you need some guidance, here's what the experts say: The shape of your *face* should determine the style of the glasses. In general, the frame shape should *contrast* with your face shape, and the glasses size should be in proportion to your face size.

Triangular

Round

Oval

Heart-shaped

Squarish

What's the basic outline of your face? Here are the five standard shapes, along with the usual recommendations for frames that will make you look your best:

- **Triangular.** Widest at the jaw, narrower forehead. *Glasses:* Choose frames that are slightly wider than your jawline, to balance your face. Something fancy on the top of the frames (a thick top edge, cat-eye frames, detailing) also helps balance your broad jaw.

- **Round.** Rounded forehead, round chin, soft jawline. *Glasses:* Choose squarish or rectangular frames. You want to add angles, preferably wider than tall. Avoid round frames and oversize ones.

- **Oval.** Narrow forehead and tapered chin. *Glasses:* Any style except oversize ones.

- **Heart-shaped.** Wide forehead, narrow chin. *Glasses:* You're supposed to minimize the width of your forehead. So avoid top-heavy, wide-top, or cat-eye frames.

- **Squarish.** Wide forehead and cheeks, broad chin or strong jawline. *Glasses:* You want to soften the angles of your facial structure by adding curves, so round lenses work well. Avoid boxy or top-heavy frames. Try frames that are wider than your face's widest point.

# Chapter 5:
# Out and About

Once you're well dressed and well fed, you're all set to *go* somewhere. You'll save time, frustration, and effort if you take the following tidbits with you.

---

## Your phone's camera as memory supplement

You probably think of your cell phone's camera as a tool for *taking pictures.* That would be a reasonable assumption.

But truly savvy participants in life treat that thing as a memory supplement. Use it to take *temporary* pictures, which you'll consult maybe once before deleting them.

The number of situations when it's useful to record a scene for *temporary* reference is staggering; the hard part is just getting into the habit. For example, you should take a picture of:

- **The sign over your parking-garage space,** so you remember where you left the car

- **Something you're lending to a friend** (posed with the friend), so you'll remember who has it

- **Your open refrigerator before you go shopping,** so you won't have to wonder if you're out of milk, ketchup, bread, or whatever

- **The scratches and dents on a car you're renting,** so if they later accuse *you* of scraping it up, you'll have evidence to the contrary

- **The cable connections behind your computer or TV before unplugging them,** so you'll remember how they went when you reassemble them later. (Useful when you're moving—or moving just your TV or computer.)

- **A taxi's license** (either the license plate or the driver's license posted inside the cab), so you'll be able to track down stuff you left behind

- **Your valet or coat-check ticket,** so you'll have the number in case you lose it

- **Your children at the entrance to the amusement park,** so that if you get separated, you can show the security people exactly what they were wearing

- **The phone number or Web address on a poster or business card,** so you'll have it for reference later

- **Your luggage as you check it at the airport,** so you'll have a picture to show people if it gets lost or damaged

Phone photos are fast and easy to take, cost nothing, and take up very little space. In certain situations, including *life,* they make the perfect memory supplement.

# Teach bike riding by coasting down a hill

From the dawn of two-wheeled civilization, we've taught our children to ride a bike the same way: by holding onto the back of their bikes, running frantically beside them, bent over, shouting encouragement.

The problem here is that the poor kid has to learn too many things simultaneously: balancing, pedaling, and steering.

Training wheels have their own problems. They don't actually teach the hard part—balancing—so they don't really give much of a head start to the learning process.

There is, in fact, a better way: the grassy-hill method. Ready?

Lower the seat so that your little rider can reach the ground with both feet.

Start partway up a gentle grassy hill. Encourage her simply to lift her feet about an inch—and then coast down the hill. She can use her feet to control her speed if she likes. Repeat a couple

of more times, periodically moving higher up the hill. Liberally sprinkle with praise.

See how you're teaching her first to balance, without having to worry about steering and pedaling?

After a few runs, let her try coasting down the hill with *one* foot on a pedal. Then two.

Everyone still alive? Finally, she's ready to try *turning* the pedals—partway down the hill.

You can probably predict the final steps: Little by little, raise the seat toward its ideal position. Teach starting up from a *flat* surface (start the pedal at the two o'clock position as you face the bike, where it's easiest to push down).

And when you're ready for your first bike ride together, see to it that ice cream is involved.

-------------------------------------------------------------

# Get your picnic drinks cold

Ever since the first caveman went to the first company picnic, we've been putting ice into picnic coolers to keep our food cool.

That's fine if the cooler's contents are meat and cheese. But if it's drinks, such as soda or beer, you might want that cooler to get cooler. You might want it *cold,* or even *ice* cold. And you might want it to get cold *fast*.

If you simply put ice into the cooler, you'll be disappointed: It will never get colder than, say, a refrigerator. To be exact, your cooler can never get any colder than the melting point of ice: 32 degrees.

It is possible, though, to get your drinks colder than that—ice cold, as they say, which (according to Michelob) is perfect for beer. The trick is to *salt your ice water.*

Funny thing about salt: It lowers the freezing temperature of water (from 32 degrees down to about 15), which is why we use it on our sidewalks to melt ice in the winter. Salt water can remain a liquid at lower temperatures than regular water. That's why you add salt to the ice in an ice cream maker, for example.

So here's the trick: Dump a cup or two of salt into the cooler; mix it with the ice. Table salt, rock salt, and what's sold as "ice cream salt" or "sidewalk salt" all work.

The water will quickly become super-cooled, and so will your drinks. That's partly because of the frigid water, and partly because your bottles or cans are *covered* in water. If they were in there with ice cubes, not all of the can or bottle would be touching the ice.

(The melted water will be salty, of course—so don't forget to wipe off your can before putting your lips and tongue on it.)

In any case, this trick can even semi-freeze your soda, making it deliciously slushy. This trick also works great for quick-chilling a watermelon—or a bottle of white wine or Champagne. —*Robert Christensen*

--------------------------------------------

# The right way to use your bike's gears

After a couple of rides on your new bike, you'll figure out which direction to move your gearshift lever for higher gears (better power going down hills) and lower ones (easier pedaling up hills).

When you're at a dead stop, of course, you usually want a lower gear, so that it's easier to start pedaling forward.

But the only time you can shift a bike's gears is *while it's moving.* So most people shift into the lower gear when the light changes and they start up again. Trouble is, you're starting off in your *previous* gear (a high one for high speeds) and trying to shift into a new one from a dead stop. The result is a clacking, wobbly, gear-stressing moment that's bad for both your bike and your public image.

The best time to shift into a low gear is just *before* you come to a stop, while you're still in motion. When you take off again, you'll find it comfortable and stable, and you'll look like a pro.

--------------------------------------------

# How to read your tablet with sunglasses on

Polarized sunglasses do something weird to iPads and some other tablets: They make its screen appear totally black.

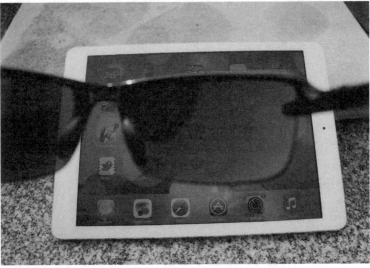

But a funny thing about polarization: It blocks glare in only one dimension. In other words, if you turn your iPad 90 degrees (so it's wider than tall), the image returns!

# Stores that don't require return receipts

From the beginning of time, visitors to physical stores have been told, "Save your receipt in case you need to return it!"

But we live in the modern, advanced, digital age! Surely a store's *computer* can remember what we bought.

And sure enough: The truly enlightened store chains are happy to accept a return or an exchange without your having to bring the receipt.

For your shopping reference, here's what happens at the most enlightened big-name stores when you return an item without the receipt:

- **Ann Taylor.** Store credit.

- **Apple.** Full refund.

- **Banana Republic.** Store credit.

- **Best Buy.** Store credit.

- **Costco.** Full refund.

- **CVS.** Store credit.

- **Home Depot.** If you used a credit card, full refund; if cash, store credit.

- **Kohl's.** Store credit.

- **Lands' End.** Store credit.

- **Lowe's.** If you used a credit card, full refund; if cash, store credit.

- **Macy's.** If you used a credit card, full refund; if cash, store credit.

- **Office Depot.** Store credit, and no returns of electronics.

- **Radio Shack.** If you used a credit card, full refund; if cash, store credit.

- **Staples.** Store credit.

- **Target.** Store credit.

- **T.J.Maxx.** Store credit.

- **Walgreens.** Store credit.

- **Walmart.** Cash if under $25, store credit (gift card) if over $25.

Note that your opportunity to return stuff usually expires after 2 weeks, a month, or 90 days, depending on the store—so decide you're unhappy fast.

-----------------------------------------------------------

# What you need to know about extended warranties

Extended warranties are almost *never* worth buying.

That's the conclusion of Consumer Reports, which has been tracking product failure rates and extended-warranty programs for years.

When you pay extra to extend the warranty period on your car, phone, washer, fridge, or microwave, you're placing a bet that it will fail. But they almost never do—and when they do, it usually happens within the original warranty period (for example, the first year you own it).

Still, 40 percent of refrigerator buyers spring for the extended warranty, a victim of emotion and salesperson pressure. (The salespeople usually get a commission for selling you these warranties.) The emotion in question is guilt: You're afraid that if the machine does break when it's out of warranty, you'll feel terrible that you didn't get the extended warranty when you had the chance.

There are a few exceptions: used cars, for example, and extended warranties on mobile gadgets (like laptops and phones) that cover *everything,* including loss and dropping.

In general, though, extended warranties are a waste of money.

-------------------------------------------------------------

# Shift your credit card due date

If you're a loyal consumer soldier, you pay off your credit card bill every month. You're probably used to paying it off whenever the card company says it's due—maybe the 12th of the month, or the 20th, or whatever.

But did you know that the monthly due date is *up to you?*

You might want to shift it to the first of the month, to make it easier to remember. Or you might want to shift your Visa card so its due date is separated farther from your AmEx due date. Or maybe you want them all due on the *same* date, for simplicity.

All you have to do is ask. Call the credit card company's customer-service number and tell them the date you want; it shall be yours. —*Sara Solnick*

# How to find the 800 number

Next time you need to find the customer-service number or email address for some company, don't waste time on its Web site. That's a recipe for frustration; a lot of companies bury their contact information or leave it out altogether.

Instead, just Google it. Search for "netgear support" or "avis customer service email" or "mcdonalds 800 number," for example. You'll be shocked at how easy it is to find this information this way.

Or visit www.contacthelp.com. It's a free Web site that maintains an up-to-date database of the customer-service contact information of the world's companies: email, phone, Web site, hours of operation, and so on.

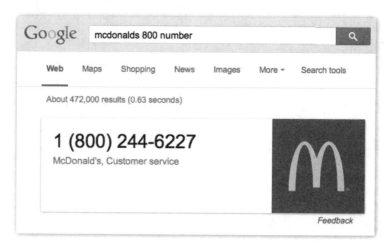

# Chapter 6:
# House and Home

After a hard day of getting dressed, driving, working, and shopping—well, after a day made *less* hard by the secrets revealed in this book—there's nothing like coming home to your own sanctuary.

But even here, in the rooms you know so well, there are lessons to be learned, and tasks to be performed more efficiently. Here they are: a collection of accumulated home shortcuts, ranging from saving money on utilities to a few handyman specials.

- - - - - - - - - - - - - - - - - - - - - - - - - - - - - - - - - - - -

## The money your hot-water heater is wasting right now

It costs money and energy to heat your home's water, right?

Right. Therefore, if you're heating your house's water hotter than you can stand in the shower—and you probably are—you're wasting money and energy.

Examine the temperature handle on your shower. If it's not turned *all the way up* to the HOT position, you're wasting money.

Go into the basement, laundry room, or wherever you keep your water heater. Turn its thermostat down a bit. Most manufacturers recommend keeping it between 120 and 140 degrees Fahrenheit—but even 120 is probably hotter than you really need it.

It may take a couple of showers before you figure out the sweet spot. But your newly lowered gas, oil, or electric bill will give you a warm feeling indeed.

And now that you've learned how to adjust your hot-water heater, remember to turn its temperature down before you leave on vacation. No point in heating up water for an empty house.

# A quick scissor-sharpening trick

Cut through a piece of sandpaper a few times. Insta-sharpening for your scissors!

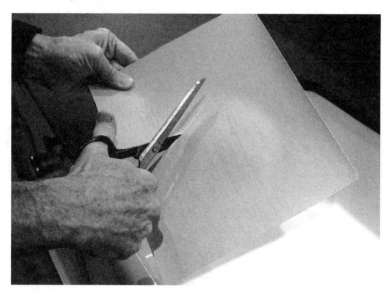

# Fight back against the razor industrial complex

You've heard the old saying "Give away the inkjet printers; sell the ink cartridges"? Nobody's taken that to heart more than the razor industry. Today's razor-blade cartridges are incredibly expensive—$30 for a dozen Mach 3 cartridges, for example—and the blades are engineered to need replacing incredibly soon.

According to Gillette, you'll have to throw away that precious cartridge after only five weeks. According to actual men shaving, it's even sooner. In fact, most people discover that they get a really close shave from a blade only the first *couple* of shaves.

But here's the shocker: The shaves don't get worse because your blade is getting *dull*. Your shaves get worse because the blade is getting *rusty*.

When you leave a wet blade out in the air, the metal oxidizes—it rusts microscopically. Soon thereafter, the weakened metal edge begins to flake, and presto: rough, dull shaves.

If you could eliminate that reaction, you'd be able to make your cartridges last a *lot* longer.

You can. Just *dry the razor completely* after each shave. You can do that in a couple of ways:

- **Use a blow dryer or a fan.**

- **Shake off the water,** and then swish the razor head in rubbing alcohol. (Use a small flip-top plastic storage container for the alcohol.) Alcohol blasts away the water molecules and then evaporates very quickly.

Drying the blades makes them last at least three times as long; some people report making them last *much* longer. Months.

-------------------------------------------------------

# Unify your soaps and save money

Pity the bar of soap. Its life path consists of shrinking away, shower after shower, becoming thinner and smaller until nobody can grip it in the shower anymore. And then it winds up in the landfill.

Savvy showerers, however, have devised a better way. When a bar of soap becomes nothing more than a sliver, squish it (while it's wet) against a new bar of soap (while it's wet). The two soaps merge into a single glorious block, and you go right on making yourself clean. You save money, goop, and landfill space.

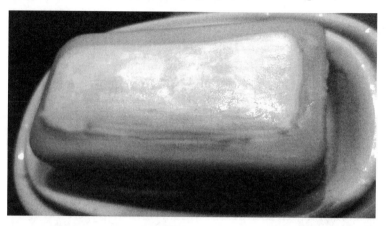

# The old shattered-lightbulb potato trick

Every now and then, a happily installed lightbulb shatters. It's a common side effect of having children who throw balls around indoors.

Or maybe you try to change a burned-out bulb—but because it's been installed for a long time, it has corroded into the socket, and it shatters when you try to unscrew it.

And now there's nothing remaining but the jagged, sharp, broken-glass edges of the metal lightbulb base, which is extremely difficult to remove.

If you ask the nearest grandpa, he'll probably tell you to use the old half-a-potato trick.

- **The old half-a-potato trick.** First, *turn off the power to the light socket.* Turn off the corresponding circuit breaker, if you can figure that out. The potato will not protect you from current that's still flowing.

Now cut an Idaho potato in half. Dry it off completely, especially the cut side.

Gripping the rounded skin portion, press the cut surface of the potato into the amputated lightbulb. At this point, you should be able to unscrew the bulb's base, using the potato as a handle.

The problem with the old half-a-potato trick is that, unless you're careful, it can leave potato juice behind. That could lead to more corrosion and a repeat of this whole nightmare down the line.

That's why you'll never catch an electrician using half a potato. Instead, here's the less fun but more professional method:

- **The needle-nosed pliers method.** Grip the exposed metal of the bulb's base with needle-nosed pliers and manually unscrew it that way. You may wind up bending the bulb's base, but that's totally fine. You won't be needing it for anything.

And, for heaven's sake, come up with some rules for indoor sports around here.

----------------------------------------

# Vegetable oil for better shoveling

If you coat your shovel's blade with nonstick cooking spray, you'll find that snow doesn't stick to it between shovelfuls. More efficiency, less backache.

----------------------------------------

# The great rubber-band paint-can trick

When you're painting a house or a room, you spend a lot of time dipping your brush into the paint can. Most people wipe off the excess on the edge of the can after each dip. Trouble is, that gunks up the rim of the can (where you'll have to tamp the lid back on later) and often results in paint dripping down the outside of the can.

A much better idea: Bisect the can's opening with a rubber band or a piece of duct tape. Wipe your brush on *that* after each dip.

You'll keep both the can rim and the can outside clean and paint-free.

---

# Vampire power: The Basics

Have you heard of vampire power? No? Then how about standby power, standby loss, or idle current?

It all refers to wasted energy. When you leave something plugged in when you're not using it—your cell phone charger, for example, or your microwave—it generally consumes a trickle of electricity. Add it up across America, and it turns out to be a *lot* of electricity: $10 billion worth, according to the EPA.

You're paying for part of that, of course—your cable box alone runs you $18 a year in vampire power, or $34 if it has a DVR, too. And the Earth pays for the power that must be generated to fuel all of it.

Some devices—TVs and stereos, for example—have to stay on, "listening" for someone to press the remote control's ON button. Computer peripherals, such as printers and scanners, keep one eye open just in case your computer sends them a signal. Hundreds of gadgets remain in standby mode so that their clocks or status gauges remain up to date.

There are only a few steps you can take to fight back:

- Unplug things that don't need to be on, or plug them into a power strip that's easy to switch off. Don't leave your chargers plugged in.

- Buy a Kill-A-Watt meter (about $18). You can plug a device into this meter to find out exactly how much juice it's using, when in use or when *not* in use.

- Buy power strips that use a master-slave arrangement: When you turn off the main appliance (like the TV), the associated outlets (such as the Blu-ray player and sound bar) cut power. Other power strips can cut power to outlets based on time of day or the absence of motion nearby (meaning you're out of the house).

-----------------------------------------------------------------

# How not to lose the end of the tape on the roll

Don't you hate it when the end of a roll of tape somehow disappears into the roll? You claw and claw with your fingernail, but it doesn't come up easily; maybe it even shreds.

This is a tiny, *tiny* life problem, to be sure. But then again, it takes only a tiny, *tiny* amount of effort to prevent it.

Before you put the tape back in the drawer each time, stick *something* to the end of it. A paper clip, a penny, a toothpick, a bread-wrapper tab. Or just fold the end of the tape under itself.

Your poor fingernail will never have to dig again. At least not into tape.

---

# Sleep: The Basics

According to the Centers for Disease Control and Prevention, sleep deprivation is now officially a public-health epidemic. Half of Americans say they don't get enough sleep. And studies make it clear that sleep deprivation is a disaster. It leads to car accidents and industrial accidents, and makes you more likely to develop hypertension, diabetes, obesity, and depression. Fun stuff.

How much sleep are you supposed to get? According to the National Institutes of Health, school-age children need at least 10 hours of sleep a night. Teenagers, 9 or 10. Adults, 7 or 8.

Here, all in one place, is the master list of what science has shown to help or harm your chances of getting decent rest.

- **Consistent hours.** Whenever possible, go to bed at the same time each night; wake the same time each morning.

- **Food.** A big meal right before bed will make it harder to fall asleep.

- **Coffee, cola, nicotine.** They're all stimulants. Take them close to bedtime, and you'll stay up.

- **Alcohol.** Alcohol may make you drowsy, but it also triggers alpha-wave activity in your brain, which disrupts the *quality* of your sleep.

- **Heat.** You sleep best in a cool room.

- **Noise and light.** If street noise or light keeps you up or wakes you early, it's worth making some serious effort to seal off your eyes and ears. The cheap way: foam earplugs and eye masks. The better way: Make your bedchamber darker and quieter. Shades. Window noise-reduction treatment.

- **Exercise.** It might not seem to make sense—doesn't exercise get you pumped up?—but exercise during the day makes it easier to fall asleep at night. (Unless it's right before bed—then it *does* pump you up.)

- **Hot bath.** The bath itself relaxes you. Then, when you get out, your body temperature drops, which is an on-ramp to sleepiness.

- **Naps.** Short naps are fantastic for making up for lost sleep—but avoid taking them late in the day. You'll use up your sleep juice and have trouble falling asleep again.

- **Electronics.** There's a new threat to sleep. The latest studies have established that the blue light from the screens of smartphones, tablets, and laptops interferes with your brain's production of melatonin, the hormone your brain associates with nighttime and sleep. If you have trouble falling asleep, eliminate screens near bedtime.

If you've violated some of those golden rules—or if you're just super stressed lately—you may still have trouble getting to sleep. In that case, here's one final golden rule:

Don't lie awake for hours. If you haven't gotten to sleep in 20 minutes, get up and do something else—something calm—until you feel sleepy or until you think it's worth another shot. That's because lying there awake gives you anxiety about lying awake, which makes you lie awake, which gives you anxiety....

# Your two secret bonus screwdrivers

Check in the tool drawer of a typical home, and you might well find a four-in-one screwdriver. That is, it comes with four different tips (bits) that snap into the shaft—a flat head, a Philips head, and so on—so that a single handle can manipulate four different kinds of screws.

What you may not realize is that your four-in-one screwdriver is actually *six* in one. The shaft itself has the same opening size as 1/4-inch and 5/16-inch nuts, meaning that you can use your screwdriver without a tip to unscrew them. You can also use the shaft without a tip to turn the most common hex-head (six-sided) screws.—*David Caleb*

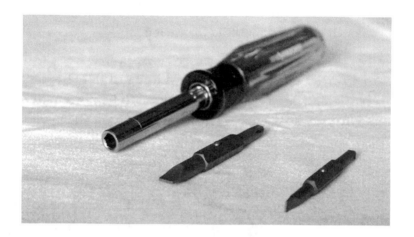

# How to deal with a stripped screw

You *strip* a screw whenever your screwdriver rips apart the slots in the screw head. Maybe the screw is stuck much tighter than you anticipated, or maybe you didn't use enough pressure on the screwdriver. In any case, once the screw head is stripped, it's hard to recover.

But not impossible. Here are the solutions, in order of difficulty:

- **Put a wide rubber band** between your screwdriver tip and the screw head. Push *hard* with the screwdriver. Often, the extra grip of the rubber band is just what you need.

- **If you've stripped a Phillips-head screw,** try using a *regular* (flat-head) screwdriver of the right size. Add the rubber band if necessary.

- **With a hammer, gently tap** the screwdriver into the screw. Often, this technique buries the screwdriver tip just deep enough into the screw head to give it grip.

- **Use a screw extractor.** It's an inexpensive, specialized screwdriver (or screwdriver bit) with special threads on its very strong metal tip. They're supposed to burrow into the screwdriver head, once again giving you enough grip to start turning.

If all else fails, you can always just bulldoze your building.

# How to stop your garbage can from riding up with the bag

Do you use plastic bags to line your trash can? Do you have to hold the can down with your feet when you're pulling the bag out? Are you ready to solve a First World problem?

The problem, of course, is suction. You're trying to pull a full bag of trash out of a plastic garbage can, so you're creating a vacuum beneath it, which makes the trash can want to stay married to the bag.

The solution is to make a couple of airholes in the side of the trash can. (Use a drill, or a knife, or heat up the tip of a Phillips-head screwdriver so that it melts its way through the plastic.)

Make the holes in the back (so you won't have to see them) and partway up (so the trash can won't leak if garbage juice drips to the bottom).

# Can opener for blister packs

Americans can't all agree on much, but this much is unanimous: That infernal hard, clear plastic packaging—sometimes called a "blister pack"—is darned hard to open. Those packages are designed to present their contents to shoppers, while simultaneously frustrating shoplifters. Only trouble is, they also frustrate *you* when you buy the thing and try to get it open. It's useless and dangerous to open those blister packs with bare hands, scissors, or knives.

The *best* way to open them is with the Open X, a $10 tool designed expressly for opening those packages (myopenx.com).

But if you don't have the patience or the 10 bucks, here's the homemade version: You can open those packages with an ordinary can opener. Just use it to pierce the flat edge of the package and turn the handle, exactly as if you're opening a can.

# Happiness: The Basics

In theory, happiness is what we're about, right? Every decision we make, at some level, boils down to trying to be happy.

But when researchers actually *study* happiness, they find some surprising quirks.

For example, you might suppose that great news like winning the lottery, dropping 20 pounds, or getting a new job would make you happy. And it does—briefly. But it's only a spike. (If that *sentence* makes you less happy, then consider this: The opposite also is true. Bad external events make you unhappy—but that, too, is just a dip. Then you return to your usual self.)

If you need more convincing: A University of Massachusetts study found that people who'd been suddenly paralyzed in an accident were *more* hopeful in their outlooks than people who'd just won the lottery.

So what *does* bring happiness—from a brain-science perspective?

Lots of factors are beyond your control. Happy people are often optimistic, spiritual, extroverted, and compassionate, have a great sense of humor, and come from happy parents. Lots of their happiness, in other words, was just handed to them by their genes or upbringing.

But there *are* some happiness factors that *you* control—factors that produce *long-term* happiness. Here's what the research has concluded on this front:

- **Companionship.** Overall, people who spend more time with friends and loved ones are happier than people who are solitary. Feeling isolated lets feelings of insecurity and self-doubt blossom.

- **Control.** Here's one definition of depression: A sense that you have no control over your circumstances. In studies of nursing-home patients and prison inmates, having control over simple things such as furniture placement and selecting TV channels produced measurable improvements in morale and alertness.

  When things are awful, it helps to find things you *can* control, even if they're little things. Join a book club—your idea, your initiative. Purge your closet. Binge-watch a TV show all day Sunday. Do small things that *you* chose to do.

- **New things.** Trying new things has two effects. First, it releases dopamine (the "happy drug" in your brain).

  Second, it makes your life seem longer! You know how coming *home* from a new place always seems to be faster than *going* there? Same idea. Time slows down during new experiences and accelerates during repetitions.

- **Exercise.** The science of this one is well established. Physical activity releases endorphins and serotonin in your brain—chemicals that make you feel good and love life.

- **Sleep.** Predictable, really. When you're exhausted, it's very hard to feel upbeat.

- **Do-gooding.** Volunteering, giving a gift, sending a note of praise to someone—all of these selfless gestures give you a connection to other people and make you feel good about yourself.

Finally, one more thing about built-in qualities like optimism, humor, and extroversion: Some studies indicate that people who *fake* these qualities often experience the same increased happiness as people who *naturally* exhibit them. (This example is from *Psychology Today*: "You're in a testy mood, but when the phone rings, you feign cheer while talking to a friend. Strangely, after hanging up, you no longer feel so grumpy.")

So when all else fails, *pretend* to be happy; after a while, it can become real.

# Chapter 7: **Animals**

People aren't the only living, breathing things walking in and out of your life; critters count, too. There's also quite a bit of wisdom involved in mastering *them*—especially pets and bugs, as you're about to discover.

------------------------------------------------------------

## How not to have an annoying mooch of a dog

Your dog may look up at you with big, round, plaintive eyes as you sit down to dinner. He may put his warm, soft muzzle on your thigh. He may wag his tail pleadingly. How can you resist tossing him a scrap of food?

*Don't do it.* Once you feed your dog, you've actually *trained* him that begging will get him food. Every time you sit down to eat for the rest of your life, he'll come and beg and bug you.

On the other hand, if you *never* reward his begging, he'll stop doing it. You and he will both be a lot happier.

# How to avoid losing your pet forever

If your dog or cat is pretty much an indoor pet, there's no more terrifying moment than the one where you discover that he has slipped outside and is nowhere in sight.

Out you go with flashlights, calling his name through sobs, wishing you had a chance to do things over.

Well, you do. Go to the vet *this week* and get an ID microchip implanted in your dog or cat.

It's about the size of a grain of rice; for about $45, your vet will inject it under your pet's skin. (It doesn't hurt.) The microchip isn't GPS and doesn't require power; instead, it reveals only an ID number when someone passes a special reader wand over it. That number is stored by a central pet registry that maintains your latest contact information. (There may be a monthly charge for services such as continuous monitoring, but you don't have to pay it; ID lookups are free.)

Here's the thing: If someone finds your pet and turns it in to a vet, your town's animal-control department, or the ASPCA, they'll use that reader wand, and you'll get your pet back. Period.

If someone finds a pet that *doesn't* have a microchip (or a collar), on the other hand, you have very little chance of getting it back; for collarless cats, the odds are less than 2 percent.

------------------------------------------------------------

# Getting your cat back

If your housebound cat slips out the door, the good news is that cats aren't big on travel. Even after several days, your cat is probably still within a few houses of yours.

Begin your search around the edge of your house or building; striking out for open spaces is unlikely cat behavior. Look in every hiding place: decks, bushes, crawl spaces, stairwells, under parked cars, and so on.

If you don't have any luck right away, put up your flyers, call the neighbors, and put an ad on Craigslist, with photos. Cats hide out during the day, meaning that your best searching opportunity is at night. Use a very bright flashlight to sweep the nearby properties; look for reflections of your flashlight from the cat's eyes. Carry some cat treats to lure the cat closer once you find her.

Of course, you'll panic less if you've had your cat microchipped (page 135).

# Getting your dog back

What if the worst should come to pass, and your dog runs away? Sure, do all the usual things—calling neighbors, putting up flyers, walking around calling her name.

But you might have more luck helping the dog find *you*.

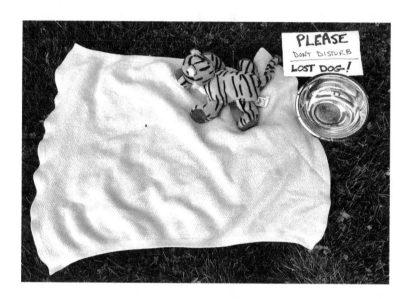

Gather up some things that smell like you—or the dog. A piece of clothing you've been wearing all day. The dog's blanket, bed, crate, or toys. Leave them at the spot you last saw your dog. Leave a bowl of water (your pup will be thirsty), but not food (which other animals will eat). And leave a note asking passersby not to disturb this setup.

Check back every day, or more than once. Incredibly, eventually, you'll return to that spot and find your best friend waiting, thanks to the miracle of scent.

# How to approach a strange dog

It should be pretty clear if a dog you're just meeting is friendly: He comes right up to you, wagging, sniffing.

If you're not sure how friendly he is, or if he's just shy, here's how a nonthreatening, inviting human behaves:

Take it slow and gentle. Crouch down (see how nonthreatening you are?). Look off to the side instead of making direct eye contact (hey, you're not trying to dominate him!). Offer him the back of your hand to sniff, and give him time to sniff it; for a dog, that's like reading your résumé.

If that ritual has gone well, give him a scratch under the chin, keeping tabs on his mood. Reaching over a dog's head to pet him there can frighten a skittish dog.

# The great pet-hair secret

If you have a dog or a cat, and it's warm out, then you also probably have pet hair on your furniture.

Sure, they sell special pet-hair lint rollers. But you know what's cheaper and easier? With a damp sponge, wipe repeatedly in the same direction, rolling the hair into a wad on the sponge. Pluck it off and toss it.

Packaging tape or wide masking tape works, too.

Both of these techniques slurp up the hair but leave the furniture in place.

# A reassuring note about bees

Bees are very protective of their queen, and of their hives. If you mess with the hive, they'll lash out and sting you.

But here's the thing: When they're *away* from their hives, they're amazingly gentle. They have absolutely no interest in stinging you. The only reason a bee would have to sting you at that point is if you threaten it—by freaking out or swatting it, which is probably exactly what your gut tells you to do.

If a bee lands on you, just hold still until it flies away. Or, if you like, blow on it. The bee will assume you're a breeze and mosey along to a less windy location.

Incidentally, here's what attracts bees to you in the first place: perfume, brightly colored clothes, sugary soda in your hand.

(If you do get stung, scrape the stinger away with your fingernail; tweezers or pinching fingers will squeeze more venom into you. Clean the sting with soap and water; apply ice; avoid scratching. Of course, if you're allergic, get medical help immediately.)

# Chapter 8:
# How to Clean Everything

L ife, as you know by now, is messy.

Not just in the jobs, relationships, and financial arenas; life is also *literally* messy. Over the years, clever homemakers and chemists have stumbled upon ingenious, efficient ways of getting things clean. Here are some of the best:

------------------------------------------------------------

## Meet oxygenated cleaners

W hen it comes to clothing stains made from organic material—grass, ketchup, blood, pet stains, juice, coffee, and so on—you should know about oxygenated cleaners (sometimes called oxygen bleach). These products, with names like OxiClean, Sun Oxygen Cleaner, and Biokleen Oxygen Bleach, release tiny oxygen bubbles that eat up organic stains and odors from fabric or carpet, and they're surprisingly effective. They're also nontoxic and better for the environment than bleach or ammonia.

You can also make your own oxygen-based cleaner to save a little money. You can find instructions online, but here's the basic recipe: You mix one part baking soda, one part hydrogen peroxide, and two parts water.

In the following tips, you'll see references to oxygen bleach; now you know what it is. (One more tip: Follow instructions. Using too much can destroy the fabric, which is even more embarrassing than just wearing grass stains.)

---

# Removing red-wine stains

The key to getting wine stains out of your clothes is, once again, cold water. Submerge the fabric in ice-cold water for a *long time*: eight hours or overnight, if possible.

That should do it. But if a faint pink stain remains, soak the spot in the usual oxygenated cleaner bath: a tablespoon of oxygenated cleaner (page 140) dissolved in two cups of very hot water. In 15 minutes, the stain will be gone. You're welcome.

---

# 57 varieties of ketchup— 1 way to remove it

So a blob of ketchup escaped your burger and landed on your shirt. Welcome to the club.

Grab a spoon or butter knife, and scrape off as much of the ketchup as you can.

Now hold the *back* of the fabric under a strong stream of cold water—the idea is to force out as much of the stuff as possible. (Yes, this generally means taking the clothing off.)

If there's any ketchupy stain left on the front, rinse it off; you'll have to call in chemical reinforcements. Immerse the stain in a solution: two cups of very hot water, one tablespoon of a powdered oxygenated cleaner (previous tip). The stain disappears, usually within an hour.

# How to get blood out of fabric

If you get blood on your clothing, furniture, or rug, the most important message is this: Rinse with cold water while it's still wet. Blood is a lot harder to get out once it has dried. (That's why you don't use *hot* water, which will help the blood set.)

A small army of devotees online swear that your own *saliva* is great for dissolving a fresh blood spot, too. (They murmur something about enzymes in your spit, but enzymes don't dissolve protein, so it must be some other effect.)

If the blood has already dried, soak in cold water first. You'll then probably need an extra hand by rubbing with either hydrogen peroxide on a cotton ball (both available at the drugstore) or, in a pinch, a paste of salt and water.

---

# How to remove hideous, unsightly candle wax

Maybe you left your candles burning too long. Maybe you were making batik or tie-dye and spilled some wax. Or you were waxing your snowboard and got it all over.

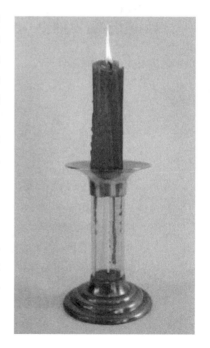

In any case, wax sometimes lands in places it shouldn't—such as the candleholder, the tablecloth, or the table itself. Here's your complete guide to removing wax:

- **Wax on the candlestick.** You can either pick away at it futilely with your fingernails— or you can pop the thing into the freezer for 20 minutes.

At that point, you can snap the wax right off. If there's any residue left, dip the candlestick in boiling water to melt it away.

- **Wax on fabric or rug.** Cover the spilled wax with part of a brown paper bag, paper towel, or a black-and-white newspaper page.

  Now set a clothing iron to medium, and iron the spot through the paper. The wax will melt and stick to the paper, lifting it right off.

  Don't use steam, and don't iron a living thing, like a person.

  If the wax is on something plastic, set the iron to very low heat—or just use a blow-dryer instead.

- **Wax on a wooden table.** Put an ice cube into a plastic bag, and hold it against the blob until the wax is hard and brittle. Now you can scrape it away with a credit card; finish up with your regularly scheduled furniture polish.

- - - - - - - - - - - - - - - - - - - - - - - - - - - - - - - - - - - - -

# Make your hands stop stinking

After you've cut or handled onions or garlic, you may notice that your hands smell like onions or garlic. (Shocker!) Doesn't seem to matter how many times you wash them.

The trick is to rub them with *toothpaste*. Not only will you eradicate the onion/garlic smell, but your hands will have fresh breath and fewer cavities.

# How to get gum off clothing

Freeze it.

Seriously, that's it. Once you've frozen the garment (and the gum), the gum pops right off.

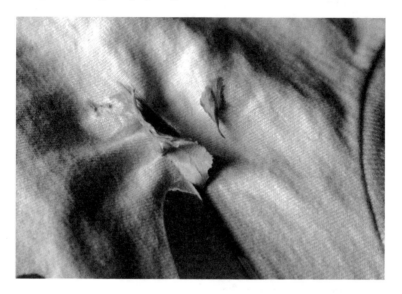

# The stainless-steel baby-oil trick

The stainless-steel baby-oil trick goes like this: Use baby oil to clean and polish stainless steel: ovens, refrigerators, stoves, and so on. It costs a lot less than stainless-steel polish, and it works like—well, like baby oil on stainless steel.

# Dry-erase marker can erase permanent marker

So some idiot drew on your dry-erase whiteboard with a permanent marker?

No problem. Dry-erase marker ink contains a strong solvent. If someone drew with a Sharpie on your whiteboard, carefully draw *over it* with a dry-erase marker. Then, while the ink is still fresh, erase it as usual, with the dry-erase eraser. (Repeat if necessary.)

Believe it or not, that's the best, quickest way to remove "permanent" ink.

---

# The trick to removing white heat marks and water rings

Guests, you know? Can't live with 'em, can't shoot 'em. They put hot dishes on wooden furniture and leave whitish heat marks. They set wet glasses onto bare wood and leave water rings.

Here's how you clean up after them:

- **Heat marks.** With a paper towel or soft cloth, rub a dab of *mayonnaise* into the wood. Use a circular motion, then wipe clean.

- **Water rings.** Believe it or not, the same mayo trick works on water rings. Small dab, rub around, wipe clean.

Coming soon: Hellmann's Real Furniture Polish.

# How to get rid of stuff

It's amazing how often you can find someone in the world willing to pay *money* for junk you're about to throw away. As you clean out your garage/attic/closet, remember that Craigslist and eBay are your friends.

If you don't have time to deal with potential *buyers,* and you're just happy to have someone haul your stuff away, check out Freecycle.org.

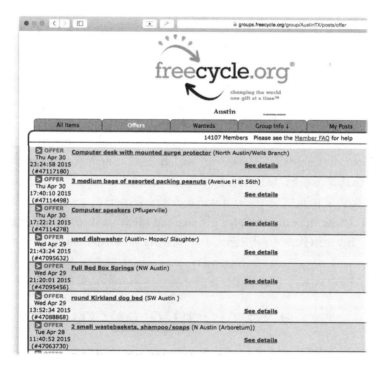

Freecycle is "a nonprofit movement of people who are giving (and getting) stuff for free in their own towns. It's all about reuse and keeping good stuff out of landfills."

It's a place to list stuff you just want to be rid of—or to look over stuff *other* people are trying to get rid of. Baby stuff, ski stuff, furniture, books, file cabinets, video games, and on and on.

And if it's *electronics* you want to unload—a phone, tablet, or laptop, for example—you want to contact a site like Gazelle .com. These outfits buy used old gadgets. Even with a cracked screen, that old iPhone is probably worth something.

------------------------------------------------

## Rubbing alcohol cleans permanent marker

Permanent-marker marks—on clothes, furniture, walls, metal, plastic, ceramic, and skin—aren't actually so permanent. Rubbing alcohol gets them off like magic.

The best bet is 90 percent isopropyl alcohol. (Most rubbing alcohol is actually 70 percent, which takes longer to evaporate.) Ethanol works, too. Even vodka if you're desperate. Or Purell (alcohol hand sanitizer) if you're *really* desperate.

Those magic juices also get tree sap off your skin, by the way. Bottom line: In the battle of Sharpie vs. Purell, alcohol wins.

------------------------------------------------

## How to clean a microwave

Put a microwave-safe bowl half full of water in your microwave; turn it on high for five minutes; wipe with a paper towel.

That's how you steam-blast the oven's walls to loosen up caked-on exploded food, like spaghetti sauce. (Some people advise adding a little vinegar, lemon juice, or baking soda—but the truth is, water alone works just fine.)

---

# The right two ways to wash windows

First of all, wash your windows on an overcast day. On a sunny day, they dry so fast that they leave streaks.

Second: Use vertical strokes on the outside of the glass, and horizontal ones on the inside. That way, you can tell which side has smudges that you've missed.

You read it here first, folks.

---

# How to recycle unrecyclable stuff

The earth's human population keeps growing, and it keeps buying stuff and throwing it away. No wonder more and more towns are getting serious about offering recycling programs.

- **Glass, metal, and paper.** These are the easy ones. All big cities, and most towns, let you recycle this stuff. Some even offer *single-source* recycling, which means you can put all of it (glass, metal, paper) into a single bin, without separating it.

- **Plastic bags.** It's rare that a city recycling program accepts plastic bags. These bags are fairly sinister, too—they take hundreds of years to decompose, and in that time, a distressing number of them find their way into the oceans, where they choke and kill fish and birds.

That doesn't mean that *you* can't recycle them. When you're finished with plastic bags, save them up. (For example, you can stuff them into *another* plastic bag that hangs from a closet doorknob.) When you've got enough to be meaningful, take them to a grocery store or other store that recycles plastic bags.

And how do you find the nearest one? By visiting http:// abagslife.com/find-a-recycle-center.

- **Electronics.** Old gadgets are pretty nasty, too. They often contain toxic metals and chemicals that can soak into the water supply. In a typical year, Americans throw about 1.8 *million tons* of electronics into the country's landfills.

Recycling them lets manufacturers reuse their expensive components, which saves a vast amount of energy and raw materials. A million cell phones contain 35,000 pounds of copper, 772 pounds of silver, 75 pounds of gold, and 33 pounds of palladium.

Here again, it's not hard to give your ancient gizmos a proper sendoff. If your junk is too old to resell, you can drop it off at any Best Buy, Target, or Radio Shack. All three chains accept and recycle old computers, GPS units, TVs, printers, monitors, cables, cell phones, remotes, headphones, and so on. Often, you'll even get an instant discount on a new purchase or a gift card. How's that for a win-win?

# Chapter 9: **Electronics**

There's an entire *book* full of basic tips and tricks for your electronics—220 of them, neatly organized into chapters like Phones, Tablets, Cameras, Computers, Email, Web Browsers, and so on.

But hey—this is no place to plug *Pogue's Basics: Tech.*

This is, however, a perfect place to offer a bonus set of tech tips. These are general, broad-appeal tips that fit right in with this book's larger topic: life itself.

---

## Press #3 to rerecord your voicemail

You're leaving a voicemail message for someone, and you mess up. Or maybe you've just said, "Dude—your behavior today was *appalling*," and you realize that a more tactful wording might be appropriate.

Or you change your mind about leaving a message altogether.

All you have to do is press the # key on your phone.

At this point, a voice gives you three options:

- **Press 1** to play your message back so you can hear it.

- **Press 2** to continue recording. (In other words, the # is a great pause key; it holds the recording while you think.)

- **Press 3** to erase your voicemail. You can start over again if you like, but you don't have to.

Impressively enough, all four US cell phone carriers—Verizon, Sprint, AT&T, and T-Mobile—treat the # keystroke exactly the same way, and offer exactly the same options when you press it.

------------------------------------------------------------

# Get all your texts when you land

Here's a little-known fact about text messages.

Ordinarily, your cell carrier (Verizon, AT&T, or whatever) tries to deliver your incoming texts immediately after they're sent. If your phone is unavailable—it's off; it's dead; it's on a plane—the carrier will try again to send the text in five minutes.

But if your phone is still unreachable then, the carrier's attempts to send that text *slow down.* It tries again after ten minutes, then after 30, then an hour. So if you fly across the country, you might have a bunch of backed-up text messages that haven't reached your phone yet, and they may not start to pour in until an hour after you've landed.

If only there were some way to tell the carrier: "I'm on the ground, and my phone is online again! Please send my backed-up messages—and resume sending new ones immediately!"

There is: Just send *yourself* a text message.

That gesture forces your phone to connect to your carrier, thereby letting it know that you're alive and online. Your pending messages come flooding in, and you'll get any *new* messages instantly.

(This technique applies only to standard SMS text messages—not to messages that come from the Internet, such as iMessages on an iPhone or BBM on a BlackBerry.)

---

## Tie a knot in the left earbud

Tie a little knot in your left earbud cord.

From now on, when you put them on, you don't have to fire up the electron microscope to hunt for the tiny L and R designations on the buds. You know by looking, or even by touching. Short, sweet, and super useful.

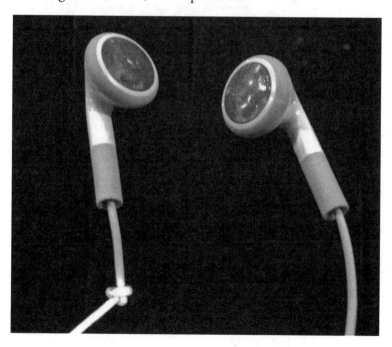

# 911 always works

Handy to know: You can dial 911 on *any* cell phone. Even one that's password-protected. Even one that's been deactivated and has no cellular plan. Even if you're in an area that doesn't seem to have cellular service!

On an iPhone, for example, there's an Emergency button right on the screen where you're supposed to enter your pass-

word. So even if it's someone else's locked phone, you can still make that call.

If you have some technophobic relatives who claim they don't need a cell phone, you could equip them with an old, out-of-service one to keep in the glove compartment. Without paying a cent, they'll always have a way of calling for help. (They'll have to keep it charged, of course.)

Oh—and in Europe, they don't have 911. They have 112.

---

# Make your phone notice the LTE network

Over the years, the cell phone carriers have steadily upgraded their networks to give your phone faster Internet speed. There were the slow, stately 1xRTT and EDGE networks—remember those? Good times. Then came 3G. Then 4G. And then the best possible cellular speed (so far), called LTE. Seeing "LTE" at the top of your phone is pure happiness. It means decent Internet speed.

Sometimes, though, your phone says "3G" up there—or, worse, the ° symbol that denotes the old 1xRTT network. Or, worst of all, "No Service."

Well, if you're a farmer in Montana, that's just life. But if you live in a more populated area, the appearance of those indicators is generally temporary. It shouldn't take much additional driving or train-riding before the LTE reappears.

Except that sometimes it doesn't. Sometimes your phone gets stuck in the slower mode—it still says 3G (and gives you 3G speed) even when you know for sure you're in an LTE area, for example. Or it says "No Service" and you know there *is* service.

The solution is to whack it in the head—metaphorically. Turning the phone off and then on again works, but it's faster to turn Airplane Mode on and off again. When it comes to, the phone notices the correct network type and gives you your speed back.

# The free cell phone service for your tween

These days, kids are asking to have cell phones at younger and younger ages. It won't be long before you'll be able to buy Pampers with Integrated Smartphone Holsters.

But a cell phone is expensive. Not just the phone but the *service*. It's hundreds of dollars a year for the privilege of calling or texting your little one. Worse, here's a news flash: Kids don't *call* anymore *at all*.

What they want to do is send texts, watch videos, play music, take pictures, surf the Web, and run apps. And they can do all of *that* with an iPod Touch.

An iPod Touch is an iPhone without the monthly bill. It does everything an iPhone does except connect to the cellular network. It gets online only when in a WiFi hotspot.

But on the flip side, owning an iPod Touch means no monthly fee, no selling your soul to Verizon or AT&T. The iPod Touch does 90 percent of what a modern smartphone does—without costing a penny for the service. Chances are very good that your kid will be perfectly happy with this pseudo–cell phone, at least until, say, ninth grade. Your savings: About $900 a year.

# Label your power cords

You know that rat's nest of cables and cords that snake down from your TV or computer into a power strip or multi-plug outlet?

And you know how frustrating it is to figure out which plug goes to which device? You have to slide your fingers from the plug, up the cord, and through the tangle until you trace the cord back to its origin.

That's why, on the next free Saturday afternoon you get, you should label them. Those square plastic tabs that hold bread wrappers shut work well. So do clothespins, or even tape folded back on itself.

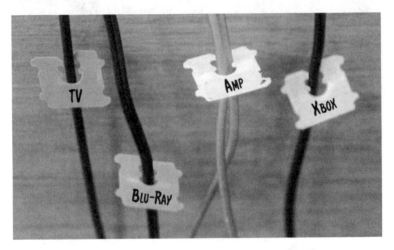

In each case, the main idea is to *label* those tabs, pins, or tapes, so that from now on, when you're down on the floor among the dust bunnies, you'll know what you're unplugging.

# Turn off the "soap opera effect"

There you are, beaming proudly at your beautiful new 95-inch HD television (or the even more modern Ultra HD television). You gather the family round, you hit the On button, call up a movie—and stare, horrified. Something's weird and wrong with the picture. It looks like *video,* like it was shot with a camcorder. It looks like a soap opera.

Welcome to the "soap opera effect." Almost all new TV sets exhibit it. It makes *The Godfather* look like it was shot on the set of *General Hospital.*

The TV companies *think* they're doing you a favor. This electronic processing is supposed to eliminate the blurring of objects that move quickly across the screen. It does that by automatically generating new frames of video *between* the ones of the original film. That's what makes the result look so bizarrely, unnaturally crispy.

If you burrow into your TV set's menus, you won't find anything to turn off called Soap Opera Effect—because that's not what it's called. Its name varies by manufacturer, but it usually includes the word Motion.

On Samsung TVs, it's Auto Motion Plus. On LG sets, it's called TruMotion. On Sony models, it's MotionFlow.

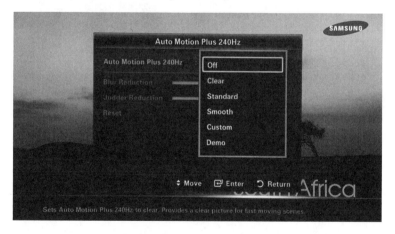

In any case, that's the setting to turn off to get your fluid cinematic look back again.

# Bringing an inkjet cartridge back from the dead

You already know that inkjet ink is among the most expensive liquids you can buy—far more expensive per gallon than ink, champagne, or perfume. So it must make you crazy when your computer reports that your ink cartridge is empty when you're right in the middle of printing something—especially when you can *see* that there's still ink in there!

Often, you're not really out of ink. Instead, dried ink has clogged the cartridge's nozzle. The quick fix: Remove the ink cartridge and heat it up with a hair dryer for a couple of minutes.

As it warms, the thickened ink flows more easily through the tiny cartridge holes. If you now reinstall the reanimated cartridge, you can enjoy a few more pages' worth of printing. Maybe celebrate by chugging a glass of Chanel No. 5.

# How to tell if your USB connector is upside-down

USB, man. That Universal Serial Bus connector has become—universal. Every computer built in the past 15 years has USB jacks. Into them, you can plug printers, scanners, cameras, phones, tablets, speakers, and on and on.

USB can be frustrating, though, because you can plug the jack in only one way, and there's no obvious, universal way to tell which side is up.

Many USB jacks display the forked USB logo on one side of the plastic—the *top* side. But not all of them.

Here, at last, is the *universal* solution to that problem: Only one side of the metal USB connector itself has a line going down the middle. That's the *bottom*.

Every time.

*Bottom (seams)*  *Top (smooth)*

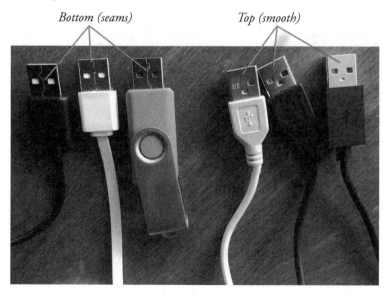

# Meet USB-C

In early 2015, the world began its long, slow introduction to one of the best cables ever designed: USB Type C.

It's a brand-new kind of connector, years in the making, concocted by a consortium of Google, Apple, and others.

USB-C is full of advantages that leave older cable designs in the dust:

- **It's tiny, so it can be built into phones or tablets.** It's the same size as micro USB.

- **It does everything.** It's a power-cord jack, *and* a video-output jack for projectors or second monitors, *and* a traditional data-transfer jack like regular USB. With the right adapter, it can even do all of that *simultaneously.*

- **Both ways are right-side up.** You never fuss with which way to plug it in.

- **Both ends are the same.** You don't even have to figure out which *end* to use.

And here's the biggest deal of all—are you sitting down?

- **They're all interchangeable.** You can use a Samsung phone charger on an Apple laptop, or a Dell laptop charger on a Google Chromebook. We have entered the era of *universal power chargers,* thanks to their delightful ability to adjust the voltage intelligently when plugged in.

In the short term, of course, it's going to be a mess. No existing USB devices will fit into USB-C jacks without adapters, and no USB-C cables will fit into old USB jacks without adapters. And the adapters aren't cheap, at least at first.

But to be alive in an age where there's only one, single, universal power cord across every gadget in the land…what could be sweeter than that?

--------------------------------------------------

# The professional photographer's light box behind your napkin

Nice restaurants *ought* to be great places for taking pictures. After all, you and your date have probably put some effort into sprucing up for the evening, and the setting is lovely.

In fact, though, it's probably dark. So to take a picture with your phone, you have two choices: (a) Allow your phone's flash to fire, which bleaches out (and blinds) your subject and turns the background into a black cave or (b) turn off the phone's flash, so you get darkness, grain, and blur.

*No flash*  *Flash*  *Soft napkin flash*

Fortunately, there's a third option: Use a second smartphone for illumination. Turn on its flashlight mode, but cover it with a napkin (cloth or folded paper). The napkin softens and diffuses the harshness of the flash. You might be surprised at how even, soft, and flattering the resulting portrait turns out.

Works great for shooting video with your phone, too.

- - - - - - - - - - - - - - - - - - - - - - - - - - - - - - - - - - - - - - - - -

# Instant email address-filling

In this life, you have to enter certain difficult-to-type blobs of text over and over and *over*—like your email address. Every form, every sign-up, every log-in—there you go, fumbling for symbols like the @ sign, typing that same doggone text over and over.

On a phone, typing your email address and phone number are especially frustrating, since you're typing on glass, on keys the size of carbon atoms.

Here's a better idea: Let your phone type them in *for* you.

Use its automatic typing-shortcut feature, which lets you set up trigger phrases (like "tyvm") to type out longer ones (like "Thank you very much!").

Set up shortcuts for:

- **Your personal email address.** Use the @@ symbol as the trigger, or the first three letters of your address.

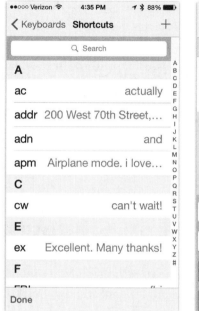 

- **Your work email.** Use @@@ as the trigger, or the first three letters.

- **Your cell phone number.** Use two colons as the trigger (::).

- **Your work number.** Three colons (:::).

On an iPhone or iPad, here's how you set this up. Open Settings. Tap General, then Keyboard, then Shortcuts. Tap the + button. On the next screen, type the expanded text into the Phrase box. In the Shortcut box, type the abbreviation you want to trigger the phrase.

On Android, open Settings. Tap Language & Input. Tap Google Keyboard, then "Text correction," then "Personal dictionary," then English. Finally, tap the + button at top right. Enter your expanded phrase ("Type a word") and the abbreviation ("Optional shortcut").

(Android phones and versions vary. On some Android editions, you find the + button by opening Settings, then Language & Input, then Personal Dictionary.)

From now on, whenever you type your abbreviation, the phone proposes replacing it with your substituted text—like your email address or phone number.

It's about time the phone started jumping through hoops for *you*.

---

# How to save an unbelievable amount on printouts

Most people who print documents at home have an inkjet printer. It can print text, graphics, and photos, quickly and easily.

Not, however, *cheaply.*

You know the old saying "Give away the razors, sell the blades"? Nobody's taken that to heart more than the inkjet-

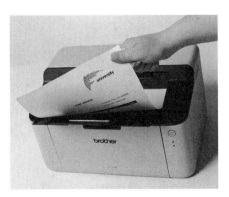

printer industry. You can buy a new inkjet printer for $30— but oh, boy, the *ink*! You think $4 a gallon is a lot for gas? A 16-milliliter black inkjet cartridge costs $18 online— which comes to $4,300 a gallon! The ink cartridges can cost hundreds of dollars a year.

Two words: laser printer.

A black-and-white laser printer is cheap ($80) and compact. It prints fast, printouts are razor sharp, and the printer lasts for years. Best of all, the toner (the black "ink" powder) is cheap and lasts a long time. It doesn't dry out, as inkjet cartridges do.

A cheap laser printer isn't any good for printing photos, of course. But for anything that can be represented by black and shades of gray, a laser printer makes a fantastic primary printer.

------------------------------------------------------------

# YouTube's universal Pause key

You probably know that you can tap the space bar to pause a YouTube video that's playing. (Don't you?)

Except that sometimes, the space bar scrolls the YouTube page instead!

It all has to do with what YouTube thinks is currently "selected"—the video, or the page. And there's no immediate way to tell which is selected.

Fortunately, you can ignore all of that confusion. Just learn to press the letter k key on your keyboard to pause the video. It works *all* the time, even when the space bar does not, whether the video is selected or not.

------------------------------------------------------------

# The Internet's best tip for laptop luggers

When you come home with your laptop, you may enjoy turning it into a more fully blown desktop workstation—by connecting a mouse, keyboard, external monitor, Ethernet cable, nice speakers, and so on.

But where are those cables lying when you're out of the house? In a seething mass, that's where.

Here's a better idea: Thread each one through the loops of a binder clip, like this:

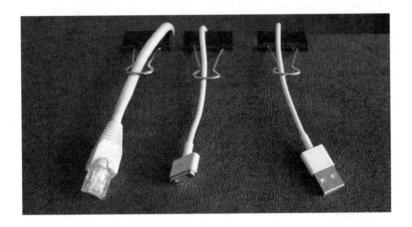

They snap onto the edge of your desk or table, and hold the ends of your cables where they're easy to grab.

--------------------------------------------------------

# The proofreading miracle of a different font

As anyone who writes or publishes can tell you, attaining a perfect proofread—ferreting out *every* typo, missing word, and so on—is staggeringly difficult. You can read over something six times, swear it's perfect—and then show it to someone else, who spots a typo instantly. Somehow, your brain gets lulled into blindness.

If you don't have the luxury of four beta readers—or even if you do—here's a miraculous trick that will make "blind spot" typos pop out: *Change the font.*

That's right. A different typeface in your word processor gives the text a different layout, with different line wraps, making it look fresh. The writing no longer looks like yours, making it easier to spot errors.

For the same reason, choosing an unfamiliar font is a great idea when you're trying to edit or shorten your paper. You're less attached to your writing, less used to its look, and more able to see something new as you read it.

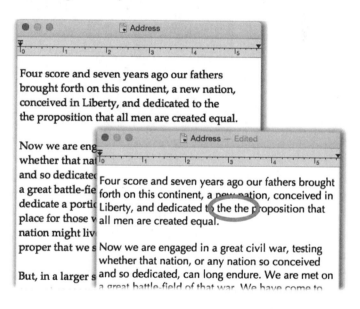

--------------------------------------------------

## Music to your pillow

If you have a recent iPhone, it came with Apple's latest earbuds, called EarPods. They come in a little plastic case.

Don't throw that case away, though—it makes a perfect pillow speaker!

When you lay the EarPods into place, that case holds their sound holes pointed upward, and keeps their cables straight and untangled. You can put the entire thing inside your pillow, connected to your phone on the bedside table, and fall asleep to music that won't bother your sleeping partner. A delightful bonus: You don't risk getting strangled by your earbud cords.

And how do you make the iPhone play you to sleep? Open the Clock app. Tap Timer. Tell the timer how long you want your sleepytime music to play. Tap "When Timer Ends," scroll all the way to the bottom, and tap "Stop Playing." Now start the music, turn the screen off, and put the phone on your bedside table. That's it: After the allotted time, the iPhone stops playing—and both of you can sleep in peace.

# Get your month's news

Have you been out of the country, out of sorts, or out of your head for a few weeks? Need a quick refresher on all the major world news you've missed?

Here's a surprising news-recap service you probably don't know about: wikipedia.org, the Internet's encyclopedia.

Do a search for *January 2016* (or whatever the month and year were). Presto: a tidy, nonpartisan, Wikipedia-style summary of all the headlines you've missed.

That trick isn't just for current events. You can type in *old* month/year combinations, too, just to get a flavor of what on earth was happening in, say, June 1973.

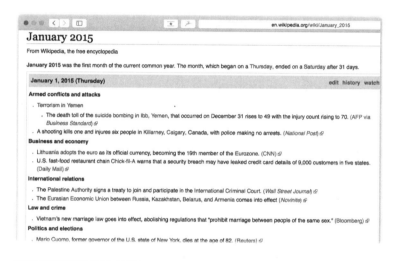

----------------------------------------------------------------

# Tech specs that make absolutely no difference

Electronics companies love to bombard you with numbers. Megapixels, gigahertz, terabytes—the more the better, right?

Well, one thing's for sure: The more, the *pricier*. A lot of these specs make absolutely no difference. You have enough to worry about when you buy gadgets—price, size, color, online reviews—without complicating your decision by measurements that won't affect you. For example:

- **Megapixels.** When you're buying a camera, you'll be asked to consider how many *megapixels* a camera takes. It's snake oil—ignore it.

  That measurement indicates how many millions of pixels (colored dots) make up each photo. It doesn't say anything about how *good* the photo is; if you want a gauge of that, comparison shop by the camera's sensor size or lens quality.

  Now, in 1997, when it was a big deal for a camera to take *2* megapixel photos, you had to worry that it wouldn't be enough for a big printout. But today, even *phones* take photos with 5 megapixels or more. You don't need to worry about resolution anymore.

- **Phone-screen resolution.** Apple, Samsung, and the other phonemakers battle one another over how many dots per inch are in their phone screens. Truth is, the screens on the world's iPhones and Galaxy phones surpassed the human eye's ability to discern individual pixels long ago. You couldn't tell the difference if you tried.

- **Processor speed.** When you're buying a laptop, it's not worth paying hundreds of dollars extra if it makes the difference between a 1.7 gigahertz Intel i5 chip (for example) and the 1.5 gigahertz model of the same chip. You will not see or feel any difference.

- **Cable plating.** Few scams are as widespread or common as the expensive-cable scheme. The industry wants you to believe that you'll get better sound from gold-plated audio cables, or better picture from $50 HDMI cables to your TV.

The plating of the audio cables makes no difference to the sound. (Why would it? The cable inside is still copper.) And cables such as HDMI and optical audio cables conduct their signals as streams of *digital* information. In other words, they either work 100 percent or not at all. The picture delivered by a $50 HDMI cable from the TV store is identical to the one from an $8 HDMI cable you found on Amazon.

----------------------------------------------------------------

# The free music "speaker" in your cabinet right now

Your phone may play music. But it is not exactly a tower of power. The force of its thundering bass won't quite knock your chair over.

That's why people buy those little rechargeable Bluetooth speakers by the shipload—to make their phones' music playback audible from farther away than arm's length.

But in a pinch, there's an emergency amplifier that gets you partway there: a cup. Or a mug.

Insert your phone into it, speaker first, and marvel at the sudden boost in volume, bass, and richness that your music gains from its new little echo chamber.

# How to find the owner of a lost phone

So some poor soul left his iPhone behind. Or someone set her Samsung Galaxy down and forgot about it.

And here you come, the Good Samaritan. The phone is protected by a password. How can you figure out whose phone it is?

If it's an iPhone, you can use Siri, the voice-activated assistant. While pressing the Home button, say, "Whose phone is this?" or "Who owns this phone?" Presto: The owner's name, address, and phone number appears. (*Usually.* It's conceivable that the person never put in his own information.)

This works on an iPad, too.

You might also try saying, "Email me" and then dictate a note; the phone's owner will get the email on his computer. You can also try saying, "Call Mom" or "Text Mom." If the iPhone knows who the owner's mom is, you're now well on your way to returning the phone.

If the phone you found is *not* an iPhone, look at the top of the screen, or the logo on the phone, to figure out which *carrier* issued it (Verizon, AT&T, T-Mobile, Sprint, or whatever). If you drop the phone off at one of that carrier's phone stores, they'll see to it that the phone and its owner are soon reunited.

Too much work? If you can make a call with the phone, press the TALK button to redial the last number called. You'll wind up calling someone who knows the phone's owner, and you can get the ball rolling.

--------------------------------------------------

# The secret keyboard shortcuts of Netflix

Lots of people watch TV shows on Netflix. And lots of people treat Netflix as though it *is* a TV—it plays, you watch.

But Netflix is a Web site, not a TV. It's interactive. And by tapping special keys on your computer keyboard, you can control the playback in some useful ways. For example:

- Tap the space bar to play or pause. You probably knew that one.

- Press the letter F to make the video fill your entire screen. (Press the Esc key to shrink the video down again, so you can see your menus.)

- Press the up or down arrow keys to make the sound louder or softer.

- Press the left or right arrow keys to skip back or forward 10 seconds.

Too bad we can't do that with *actual* TV...

---

# Learn something new 10 times a day

When you open your Web browser, what do you see? Is it some home page chosen by the maker of your computer, like Apple.com or Yahoo.com? Is it the Google search page? Is it a *blank* page?

What you see when you first open up your browser is, of course, entirely up to you; you set this up in your browser's settings (read on). But that's not the tip.

The tip here is that instead of opening the same page every time, you can learn something. You can set your home page to display a random article from Wikipedia, the online encyclopedia; or a word of the day; or a famous quotation. Why not treat yourself to a juicy brain stimulation every time you start Web surfing?

First, here's how to change your start-up page:

- **Safari.** From the Safari menu, choose Preferences. Click General. Paste the Web page's address into the Homepage box. Close the Preferences window.

- **Chrome.** Open Preferences. Where it says "On startup," choose "Open a specific page or set of pages," and click "Set pages." Paste the page's address, and then click OK.

- **Firefox.** Click the ☰ icon (top right); click Preferences, then click General. Paste the page's address into the Home

Page box. (Make sure the pop-up menu just above it says, "Show my home page.") Close the Preferences window.

- **Internet Explorer (in Windows 8).** With your mouse, point to the lower-right corner of the screen, move the pointer upward, and click Settings. Click Options, then Customize, then paste your desired page's address; hit Add.

- **Microsoft Edge (Windows 10).** Click the ⋯ symbol at top right; choose Settings. Where it says "Open with," choose "A specific page or pages." Choose Custom; paste the page's address into the "Enter a web address" box.

So what would make a good start-up page? Here are some suggestions:

- **A word of the day.** For example, http://dictionary.reference.com/wordof theday/

- **A quotation of the day.** Example: www.quotationspage.com/mqotd.html

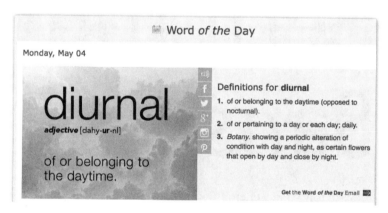

- **A random featured Wikipedia page.** Here's the link: http://tools.wikimedia.de/~dapete/random/enwiki-featured.php

# Fonts: The Basics

When the first Macintosh computer appeared, in 1984, offering a choice of typefaces to the masses for the first time, people went nuts using fonts. Every document and flyer looked like a ransom note.

You can't blame them, really. Graphic design isn't a standard course in school. How is anyone supposed to learn the rules for using fonts so that they look good—both the fonts and the people?

By absorbing the following pointers:

- **Know the two font types.** There are two kinds of fonts: *serif,* whose letters have little "feet," and *sans serif,* whose don't. See here:

# Serif font

# Sans serif

Serif fonts are generally considered more readable for big blocks of text, which is why most books and newspapers use them. Sans serif fonts are great for accompanying smaller bits of text, like headlines and captions.

- **Limit yourself.** Consider limiting yourself to *two* font families per document, maximum—maybe a serif font for the body, a sans serif font for headlines. Within each family, you're allowed to use all the variations (bold, italic, regular, etc.). But if you mix more than two font families, your flyer or ad starts to look like a ransom note again.

*Six font families*

*One font family*

- **Beware Comic Sans.** Comic Sans is a cute font that looks a little like handwriting. And it *is* cute.

# Comic Sans:
# You, too, can look like
# you're in first grade!

It's also insanely overused, to the point of being a ridiculed cliché. Consider using a different font, especially if the document is in any way meant to be taken seriously.

- **One space after a period.** Yes, yes, we know—they taught you *two* spaces when you learned to type. But that's because you (or your teacher) learned to type on a *typewriter,* and pressing the space bar didn't leave enough of a gap. They've fixed that now; in any of today's modern computer fonts, the extra space is *built in* when you press the space bar. One space, please.

# One space. It's plenty.

----------------------------------------

# Mistyped words: The Basics

Good news: Hurray! Nobody needs to know how to spell anymore! Your computer, phone, and tablet auto-correct your misspellings automatically.

Bad news: Your computer, phone, and tablet still don't know *which word you meant.* So when you type the *wrong* word, auto-correct can't do anything to help you.

Sometimes, correctness matters—when you're applying for a job, a school, or a grant, for example. Or when you're writing to somebody whose opinion counts, such as a prospective date or boss. Here, then, for your reference, are the most common switched-out words—and how to get them straight.

- **it's, its.** Use *it's* only when you mean *it is* or *it has.* "It's simple!"

  When something belongs to something else, use *its.* "Press its button!"

- **you're, your.** Use *you're* only when you mean *you are.* "You're crazy!"

When something belongs to the other person, use *your*. "That's your problem!"

- **loose, lose.** Use *loose* when something's not tied securely. "Loose change."

When you *lose* something, you can't find it. How to remember: The word has *lost* one of its *o*'s.

- **lay, lie.** Use *lay* when you're doing it to something *else*. "Lay your coat on the bed." You know that a chicken *lays* an egg, right? Same idea.

Use *lie* when you're doing it to *yourself*. "I gotta lie down."

This one's especially tricky because if it happened in the past, *lie* becomes *lay*: "Yesterday, I lay down."

And *lay* becomes *laid*: "The chicken *laid* an egg."

Confusing? You betcha. Fortunately, you don't have to remember all that. When all else fails, just remember this: If in doubt, use *lie*. Why? Because nobody ever mistakenly says *lie* when they mean *lay* ("Lie your coat on the bed" or "Yesterday, I lie down"). The mistake always goes the other direction. So if in doubt, use *lie*.

- **e.g., i.e.** These are both abbreviations for Latin phrases, so it's easy to get them mixed up.

Use *e.g.* when you mean "for example": "I like junk food—e.g., Doritos and Pringles." (How to remember: "For *eg*-zample.")

Use *i.e.* when you mean "in other words": "He ate Doritos and Pringles—i.e., junk food." (How to remember: "*in* other words.")

# How word prediction can save you time and typing

On both Android phones and iPhones (iOS 8 and later), there's a strip just above the keyboard. As you type a sentence, the phone *predicts* which word you might type next. Actually, it predicts which *three* words you're most likely to type next, and presents them to you on buttons above the keyboard.

So suppose you begin the sentence by typing, "I really." At this point, the three suggestion buttons might say *want, don't,* and *like.* You can tap one of those buttons to insert the word— and save yourself five fussy keystrokes.

But what if those guesses are wrong? What if you actually want to type, "I really *have no idea...*"?

Then just start typing *have.* The instant you type the *h,* the three suggestions might change to *h, have,* and *hope.* (One of the three buttons always shows whatever nonword you've typed so far, just in case that's what you really intend. To place it into your text, you can tap that button, the space bar, or some punctuation key.)

In other words, as you type along, those suggestions are always changing, always predicting, always using what you've typed *so far* to imagine what you're going to type next. Sometimes, it correctly guesses four or five words in sequence, which can make you grin in triumph.

The iPhone sometimes even offers several words on a single button, such as *up to* or *in the.* And if someone texts you a question ending in a choice ("Do you want aisle, window, or middle?"), the buttons offer those choices. Before you've even typed a single letter, the choices say *aisle, window,* and *middle.*

Still, if this feature is getting on your nerves, you can hide it or turn it off.

- **iPhone:** Swipe down on the button bar to hide it; you'll see it collapse into a horizontal white line. Swipe up on the white line to bring it back. Or, to turn it off fully, open Settings. Tap General, then Keyboard; turn off Predictive.

- **Android:** Open Settings, then tap Language & Input. From here, tap the name of the on-screen keyboard you use—Google Keyboard or Samsung Keyboard, for example.

  If it's Google Keyboard, then tap Text Correction, and turn off "Show correction suggestions." If it's Samsung Keyboard, turn off "Predictive text."

# The one-character phone password nobody can guess

Yes, you should have a password on your smartphone. You never know when you'll one day leave it somewhere; without a password, some ne'er-do-well can pick it up and have full access to your life.

But you probably wake up your phone 75 times a day. So having to type in a traditional hard-to-guess password every time gets *really* old. Exasperating, actually.

This is the reason some phones come with a fingerprint reader, so that you can use your finger to unlock the phone.

But if your phone doesn't have one, or it doesn't work well, here's a humble suggestion: Make up a *one-character* password—specifically, an accent character or funny symbol, such as *;* or *%* or *ſ*.

It takes only two taps to enter it (one tap to open the symbol keyboard layout, one to choose the symbol you want), yet nobody would ever guess it. (Remember, the password box doesn't give the criminal any indication of how *long* your password is.)

-------------------------------------------------------------

# When to turn off WiFi

A smartphone can get onto the Internet in two ways: over the cellular network, or in a WiFi hotspot.

*Usually,* WiFi is the way to go. Internet over WiFi doesn't use up any of your precious monthly data allowance (2 gigabytes or whatever), for which you're paying your cell phone carrier handsomely. And even if you have an unlimited-data plan, you lucky duck, WiFi connections are also usually faster than cellular ones. *Plus,* if you have Verizon or Sprint, a WiFi connection means that you can use the Internet, or apps, *while* you're on a phone call.

Sometimes, though, you'll notice that despite having a good, strong WiFi signal, your phone is struggling to get online. Maybe it has taken 90 seconds to try to open a Web page or send an email or a message. In any case, you get frustrated.

In those situations, your phone may be having *trouble* getting onto the WiFi network. Yes, it may *show* a strong signal, but that WiFi hotspot may be overloaded, frozen, protected, or otherwise not working right.

Learn to recognize those situations before you've wasted a lot of time sitting there baffled. When this happens, *turn off WiFi.* Your phone will be forced to use its cellular connection, immediately, and you'll discover that you can suddenly get online as usual.

Here's how you turn off WiFi:

- **iPhone.** Swipe up from the bottom of the screen to open the Control Center. Tap 🛜 to turn it off.

- **Android.** Swipe down from the top of the screen to open the Quick Settings bar. Tap 🛜 to turn it off. (On the latest version of Android, called Lollipop, swipe down from the top *twice* to see this bar.)

------------------------------------------------

# The "Do Not Call" list—and the "Do not send me credit applications" list

You may have heard of the National Do Not Call Registry, which "gives you a choice about whether to receive telemarketing calls at home." *Or* on your cell phone, by the way.

To sign up for this free Federal Trade Commission service, go to www.donotcall.gov. Click "Register a Phone Number," and enter your phone and cell phone numbers. (Or call 888-382-1222 from the phone you want to list.)

From now on, telemarketers are not allowed to call and bug you on those numbers. Great, right? Never say the government never did anything for you.

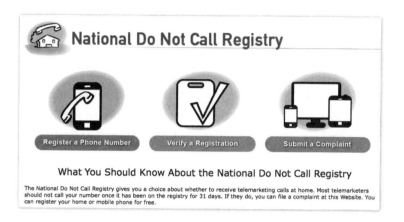

### National Do Not Call Registry

Register a Phone Number · Verify a Registration · Submit a Complaint

**What You Should Know About the National Do Not Call Registry**

The National Do Not Call Registry gives you a choice about whether to receive telemarketing calls at home. Most telemarketers should not call your number once it has been on the registry for 31 days. If they do, you can file a complaint at this Website. You can register your home or mobile phone for free.

(And if some lowlife telemarketer ignores the rule and calls you anyway, the same site offers a button that lets you report him.)

But wait, there's more. There's also an FTC list that lets you opt out of the unsolicited "preapproved" credit-card and insurance applications that arrive weekly in your mailbox, as the Brazilian rain forest slowly shrinks away to nothing.

To get onto *this* list, visit www.optoutprescreen.com, a site run by the four big credit-reporting companies (Equifax, Experian, Innovis, TransUnion). You'll be asked for some deeply personal information—name, birth date, Social Security number—to confirm that it's really you. (This is safe to provide.)

If you click Confirm, your name will be removed from those mailing lists for five years. If you also print and mail the form in front of you, they'll take you off those lists *forever.* (If you prefer to do all of this by phone, call 888-567-8688, which works out to 888-5OPTOUT.)

# The "Do Not Mail" list

If you feel that you're getting quite enough junk mail in your physical mailbox, there's something you can do about that, too.

DMAChoice is the "stop sending me junk mail" service created by the Direct Marketing Association, the trade group of junk-mailers. They've created an opt-out service in sheer terror that somebody might pass a *law* requiring them to stop the junk mail.

To sign up, go to https://www.dmachoice.org/register.php. Fill out the form, and enjoy the small reduction in the amount of junk mail the post office brings you.

# The "Do Not Email" list

That same outfit, the Direct Marketing Association, also maintains an *Email* opt-out service. It's a set of email addresses that responsible spammers agree to remove from their lists. ("Responsible spammers." Insert your own joke here.)

To add your email address to it, go to https://www.dmachoice.org/. Click "Email Opt Out Service." Fill in up to three email addresses.

Now, a word of caution: All you've done is add your name to something called the Email Preference Service—and junk-mailers aren't *required* to obey it. "You will continue to receive mail from companies with which you do business and from charitable or commercial organizations that do not choose to use eMPS," the Web site says. "In addition, you may continue to receive email from many local merchants, professional and alumni associations and political candidates."

Great.

(A much, *much* better approach to avoiding email spam is to avoid letting your email address fall into the wrong hands in the first place. Start fresh with a new email address that you use *exclusively* for email communication, and *never* type it into a Web site, ever. Not to confirm a subscription, not to receive special discounts, never. Use a different email address for Web sites. That inbox will fill up with junk, but you won't care.)

---

# What the Web-site suffixes mean

You may have noticed that most Web addresses seem to end with *.com*. There's Google.com, Amazon.com, Apple.com, Microsoft.com, and on and on.

But not all of them. You might also run across suffixes like *.gov, .org, .edu,* and so on. Knowing what they mean can be very useful, both in figuring out whose address it is and in guessing some organization's address without having to look it up.

Here's the rundown:

| Suffix | Stands for | Examples |
|--------|-----------|----------|
| .gov | U.S. government | whitehouse.gov |
| .org | nonprofit organization | pbs.org |
| .edu | schools (usually colleges) | yale.edu |
| .mil | U.S. military | army.mil |

You also might see *.net, .biz,* and *.info* a lot; those can be pretty much any kind of outfit. They're often used by companies who really wanted *.com,* but that was taken. For example, if you start a lemonade stand in Iowa but IowaLemonadeStand.com is taken, you could make your Web site IowaLemonadeStand.net.

There are hundreds of country-code suffixes, too, like these:

| Suffix | Stands for | Examples |
|--------|------------|----------|
| .ca | Canada | Amazon.ca |
| .jp | Japan | Google.jp |
| .de | Germany (Deutschland) | Apple.de |
| .eu | European Union | Microsoft.eu |

Truth is, almost anyone can use almost any suffix these days. You may run across *.tv, .city, .eat, .global,* and so on. That explosion of possibilities sometimes makes it harder to guess the address of some organization—but it will always be safe to guess that, for example, NASA's site is nasa.gov and Harvard's is harvard.edu.

------------------------------------------------

# Online scams: The Basics

The Internet is a glorious invention. It brings people together, saves us time and money, gives the downtrodden a voice.

It's also a cesspool of haters, scammers, and lowlifes.

Sooner or later, you'll receive one of these messages by email. They're very common—because, unfortunately, incredibly, some people fall for them every time. Don't be one of them.

- **The phishing scam.** You get an email from your bank (or Amazon, eBay, PayPal, Yahoo, Apple) saying that there's a problem with your account. You're encouraged to click the link to fix the problem—"or else your account will be suspended!"

If you do click the link, you go to a *fake* version of the bank's Web site. If you then "log in," you're inadvertently providing your name and password to the Eastern European teenagers who are fishing for your login information, so they can steal your identity and make your life miserable.

If you have *any* concern that the message could be *true*, do not click the link in the email. Instead, open your Web browser and type in the company's address yourself (www. citibank.com or whatever). You'll discover, of course, that there's absolutely nothing wrong with your account.

- **The mugged-neighbor scam.** "Things got out of control on my trip to London," says an email from one of your friends. "I was mugged, all my belongings including cell phone and credit card were all stolen at gunpoint. I need your help flying back home and paying my hotel bills!"

This one's especially confusing because the message comes from someone you *know*.

Needless to say, your friend wasn't actually in London and hasn't been mugged. The bad guys have planted software on your friend's computer that sent this same sob-story email to everyone in his address book.

- **The Nigerian prince scam.** "I am Mr. Paul Agabi," goes this email. "I am the personal attorney to Mr. Charles Wilson, a national of your country, who used to work with Chevron Oil Company in Nigeria, herein after shall be referred to as my client. On the 21st of April, my client, his wife and their only child were involved in a car accident. All occupants of the vehicle unfortunately lost there lives."

Turns out this rich dead guy left behind millions of dollars—and your correspondent wants *you* to have it!

If you wind up taking the bait and corresponding with this person, things will go well briefly, and you'll get very excited. But then a funny thing happens: Before you get your millions from Nigeria, you'll be asked to *send* some money to cover legal fees, bribes to officials, taxes, and other expenses. *You will never get any money.* You will be asked to send more, more, more money until you come to your senses and realize you've been bilked.

According to the FBI, this decades-old con still costs gullible Americans millions of dollars every year.

- **The preapproved credit card or loan.** Incredible! Here you are, being offered a pre-approved Visa card or loan with an impressively high credit limit. If your current financial situation isn't great right now, such an offer must sound too good to be true.

  It is. You'll send in the up-front "annual fee"—and you'll never hear from them again. There never was a credit card or loan.

  (Similar cons: "You've won a lottery!" "You've landed a great job!" "You're invited to a great investment!")

- **The Craigslist scam.** You're trying to sell something on Craigslist, the free classified-ads site—a bicycle for $300, let's say. You get an immediate offer: "Send me your address, and I will mail you check right away for $1,500 to cover the bike and shipping to me in Germany. Deposit the check and then send $450 by Western Union to my shipping company."

*Ka-ching!* And sure enough, you get a money order or certified check in the mail. Fantastic!

The only problem is, it's a forgery. You'll deposit it, send this guy $450 of your *real* money—and a couple of days later, your bank will let you know that the money order was a fake. Now you've lost your bike *and* $450.

The clues that you're being targeted: (a) The offer is for *more* than you're asking; (b) you're supposed to send your item to another country; (c) you're asked to use the other guy's shipping company.

# Chapter 10: **Your Body**

You think today's technology is complex? Wait till you start poking around the twisted, intertwined, microscopic, liquid-based, miraculous workings of your own body.

Every single day, another group of scientists releases the results of another study about health or medicine, and yet there's still so much we don't know. Much of the time, our experts are just shooting arrows in the dark. But here and there, people have stumbled onto more useful quirks of our bodies—and here they are.

- - - - - - - - - - - - - - - - - - - - - - - - - - - - - - - - - - - - - - - - - - - - - -

## Can you wake up not groggy?

According to modern sleep science, grogginess isn't exclusively a matter of not getting enough sleep. It can result from being awakened at the wrong *point* in your natural sleep cycles.

If your alarm goes off when you're in a deep sleep—REM (rapid eye movement) sleep—you feel out of it. You're suffering from what's called *sleep inertia*. It may take you an hour (or a cup of coffee) to snap out of it.

If you wake up at the lightest point of one of your natural sleep cycles, though, you feel more refreshed—even if you spent *less time asleep.*

That may seem hard to believe—surely 7 hours of sleep is always better than 6.5! But sleep inertia, and the causes of it, are real.

The question is: How do you *avoid* it?

The easy way: Don't set an alarm. Wake up when you wake up. Your body's own rhythms will take care of it.

If you must be up at a certain time (for, oh, say, *work),* there's a realm of products designed to wake you at the lightest point of your sleep cycle. Here are some examples:

- **Fitness bands.** These activity-tracking wristbands, like the ones from Jawbone and Sony, can wake you either at a specified time (by vibrating on your wrist)—*or* up to 30 minutes earlier, if that means you'll awake during a lighter phase of your sleep.

- **Smartphone apps.** You put your iPhone or Android phone beside your pillow. The app (Sleep Cycle for iPhone, SleepBot for iPhone or Android) uses the phone's motion sensors to figure out when you're asleep, and how deeply— and it tries to wake you with an alarm at the best possible moment within, for example, 30 minutes of your desired wakeup time.

- **Sleepyti.me.** This Web site tries to *predict* what time you'll be sleeping lightly—and you're supposed to set your alarm clock accordingly. It's based, however, on a 14-minute fall-asleep time and a 90-minute sleep-cycle duration, both of which are extremely variable and unreliable assumptions.

*Most* people who try the bands or the phone apps find that the theory works more than it fails: They feel less groggy when the alarm goes off, even if they actually spent less time unconscious.

------------------------------------------------------------

# Hand-washing: The Basics

It's surprising how much lore and mythology has sprouted up from the simple act of washing your hands. You're supposed to use hot water. You're supposed to wash long enough to sing "Happy Birthday" twice through. And what about Purell? Doesn't it kill bacteria just the way antibiotics do, thereby risking the rise of superbugs?

Here are the facts:

- **"Happy Birthday."** Clearly, the business about singing "Happy Birthday" twice is designed to make you spend more time washing your hands. But that's not because washing a certain spot of skin longer makes it cleaner; it doesn't.

  Instead, if you're committed to standing there for 20 whole seconds, you're more likely to scrub the parts of the hands people *miss:* your thumbs, fingernails, and the *backs* of your hands. It's not about how much time you spend; it's about how much *hands* you cover.

- **Hot water.** There's no magic to the temperature of the water. Scientists just want it to be *pleasant* so you'll wash longer (see above).

- **Purell.** Even the people who make Purell admit that washing with soap and water is the best way to clean and disinfect your hands. You're washing germs away instead of killing them.

But Purell should be your second choice if you can't find soap and water. It's basically alcohol, and it does a good job of disinfecting your skin.

Purell is also a lot better than antibacterial soap (read on).

---

## Why antibacterial soap is bad stuff

Don't buy or use soap, toothpaste, mouthwash, or other bathroom products labeled "antibacterial." For a few reasons.

- **It won't stop you from getting sick.** Cold and flu come from *viruses,* not bacteria. Antibacterial soap doesn't kill viruses.

- **It may breed superbugs.** Maybe you've heard this one: Years of overprescribing antibiotics has resulted in the rise of new, super-resilient bacteria that *nothing* can kill. The staph infection you get from these bugs, called MRSA, has become a killer in hospitals and nursing homes, to the tune of about 10,000 Americans a year. Scary, right?

  Antibacterial soap has the same problem. It contains a chemical called triclosan, which has the same problem as antibiotics: It kills *most* of the bacteria, but leaves the strongest ones behind to reproduce and get stronger.

- **Soap and water does just as good a job (and costs less).** Yes, they've studied it. Soap and water washes the germs off your skin instead of trying to kill them.

  Alcohol-based hand sanitizers like Purell are fine, by the way.

# The better way to take out contacts

Believe it or not, some optometrists and Web sites still advise you to remove your contact lenses by tugging up on the *upper* lid, as shown here. They're suggesting that you reach over your head with one arm and pull up on the lid.

It actually makes more sense (and requires less acrobatics) to tug down on the *lower* lid. After all, you're going to be grabbing the *bottom* of the lens to remove it. Isn't it more logical, therefore, to create space near the bottom of your eye?

*Wrong*                    *Right*

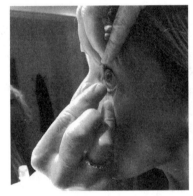 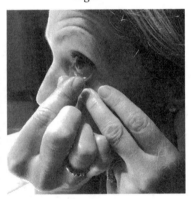

# How to make instant reading glasses with your fingers

If you need reading glasses—and if you're over 40 or so, you probably do—then the next couple of paragraphs will change your life. You're about to find out how to read small type, in a pinch, without your glasses.

Maybe you've lost or broken your reading glasses. Or maybe you don't feel like going upstairs to get them. Or maybe you're naked in the shower, frantically trying read the bottles to see which one is shampoo.

Here's the trick: Curl up your index finger, making a tiny hole. Hold it up to your dominant eye and peek through it.

Incredibly, you'll discover that the small type you couldn't read a moment ago is suddenly crystal clear! You can read the date on a penny, or the serial number on a product, or the instructions on a medicine bottle. It doesn't matter if you're nearsighted or farsighted.

So how does it work?

You're letting in only a very narrow beam of light. You're blocking the whole *cone* of light rays that, on aging eyes that don't focus perfectly, cause a spot of blur on your retina. If you know anything about photography, this might help: Your fingers are creating a very small *aperture,* like the one on a pinhole camera. And when the aperture is small, everything is in focus, near and far.

So you're turning your eye into a pinhole camera, and everything is in focus!

# How to get a splinter out

One way to get a splinter out of a finger is to dig around with tweezer tips or a needle. But that's painful, imprecise, and upsetting, especially if you're under 10.

There are better ways.

- **First resort.** Press a piece of Scotch tape against the protruding piece of splinter, and pull it right out. It works for splinters that aren't especially deeply buried.

- **Second resort.** If the splinter doesn't come out with tape, squirt a dollop of white glue (like Elmer's) or wood glue onto the splinter. Wait until it dries. Now, when you peel the glue blob away, the splinter comes out with it!

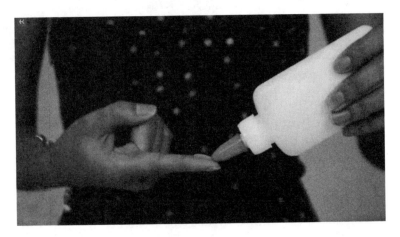

- **Alternate splinter wisdom.** If you don't have tape or glue handy, at the very least soak the finger in warm, soapy water for a few minutes. As the skin shrivels and softens, it will make the splinter's end much more visible and easier to pluck out with tweezers—or even fingers.

# The difference between Advil and Tylenol

Thank heaven for pain relievers. Without them, our headaches, sore muscles, and other aches would be a lot more… painful.

The shelves are teeming with white plastic bottles of over-the-counter medicines that promise to relieve pain. But you may not realize that (a) there are really only two types of painkillers, sold under a wide array of brand names, and (b) there's a trick to knowing which one to take when.

The active ingredients boil down to these:

- **NSAID drugs.** NSAID stands for *nonsteroidal anti-inflammatory drugs,* but of course you already knew that. The point is that there are three big NSAID drugs that all work the same way: *ibuprofen* (Advil, Motrin, Nuprin), *naproxen* (Aleve), and good old *aspirin* (Anacin, Bayer, Bufferin, Excedrin).

  These drugs treat pain, fever, *and* inflammation/swelling—so take these (instead of acetaminophen) for sports injuries, menstrual cramps, lower back pain, and arthritis. Don't take on an empty stomach.

- **Acetaminophen** ("a seat-a-MINNA-fin"). Better known as Tylenol or Excedrin Tension Headache. Acetaminophen is for reducing pain and fever; this drug doesn't reduce inflammation. It has fewer side effects than NSAIDs and is gentler on the stomach and kidneys.

Experts recommend that if you have to take a pain reliever for a long time, alternating them is a good idea. You should take all of them with a glass of water—and avoid all of them if you've had more than three alcoholic drinks. At that point, "feeling no pain" has a whole different meaning.

# The one-step trick for perfect posture

There's a lot involved in having good posture. Chest out, stomach in, shoulders back, head high, hips square…you're going to remember all that?

Fortunately, there's a single image that gets your entire self into alignment: Imagine a thread from the center of your chestbone, pulling you diagonally up.

Bingo: Chest out, stomach in, shoulders back, head high, all at once, automatically. Cool, huh?

# The easiest way to lose a couple of pounds

Go to bed.

It's true: You weigh a couple of pounds less in the morning than you did the night before. And that's *before* you go to the bathroom!

A lot of the weight leaves your body in the form of water vapor, every time you exhale—especially if your bedroom is cool. More water leaves you in the form of sweat. And water, as you probably know, is *heavy.*

You lose even more weight in the form of *carbon.* You know how we breathe in oxygen ($O_2$), and breathe out carbon dioxide ($CO_2$)? Well, during the night, you're losing about 10 billion trillion carbon atoms as you exhale—about a pound of carbon. No wonder so many people prefer to weigh themselves first thing in the morning!

The obvious follow-up question is: Aren't we *also* breathing, sweating, and expelling carbon during the *daytime?*

Why, yes—yes, you are. And you *would* lose pounds every day, just as you do at night, if it weren't for one complicating factor: food and drink. You notice the effect only at night because you stop eating and drinking during your sleeping hours.

Usually. Sleepwalkers' mileage may vary.

--------------------------------------------------------

# Read this before you get your blood drawn

If you're going to have your blood drawn for medical testing, *drink.*

No, not alcohol—water or other beverages. If you drink a lot about 30 minutes before the appointment, your blood volume increases dramatically. That makes your veins easier to find, which means that the phlebotomist (the person drawing your blood) will have an easy, quick job of sticking you. The experience for you will be a lot less unpleasant.

In a similar vein (heh), keep your arms warm before the appointment, and let them hang down at your sides beforehand. All of this keeps blood in your arms, where the phlebotomist can find it. —*Mary Margaret*

# How to get rid of belly fat

In general, as men gain weight, the fat collects around their bellies. On women, it collects on their hips and thighs. That's just how we're built.

In other words, *millions* of people have fat in these places and wish they could lose it. Here are some things that they've tried—and discovered, millions of times over, not to work:

- Spot reducing. You can do sit-ups and abdomen crunches until your stomach muscles are made of carbon fiber, but your *belly will not get smaller.* Belly fat is fat *on top* of your abdominal muscles. It's painful to accept, but true: *You cannot spot-reduce fat.*

  All you can do is lose weight *overall.* The belly fat will go away along with the rest of the weight. (This gets harder the older you get, by the way, because your metabolism slows.)

- Pills. Plenty of companies are happy to sell you supplements or other magical edibles that "burn" belly fat. Some even claim to be endorsed by TV's Dr. Oz.

  They don't work. Ever.

- Exercise equipment. The airwaves are teeming with ads for tummy bands, vibration disks, and exercise videos. All of them say they'll get rid of belly fat, because they know that millions of people will pay money for some belly-shrinking magic.

None of these things work to spot-reduce belly fat. (If they help you exercise in the name of reducing your *overall* body fat, then by all means—because that's the only way to zap belly fat.)

# Anti-itch in a pinch

You can buy all kinds of anti-itch creams at the drugstore. But when you get a bug bite or some other common itchiness and there's no drugstore visit in your immediate future, roll or rub some antiperspirant on it. The zinc works wonders to stop the itch on contact.

(Diaper-rash cream also works, for the same reason; it contains zinc oxide.)

# The Jolly Green Giant's instant ice pack

When you sprain your ankle, bang your knee, or bump your head, one of your first instincts is probably to grab an ice pack. Good move.

An even better move: Grab a bag of frozen peas. It's much less expensive than one of those actual gel packs, it molds nicely to the area needing the compress—and it'll be all thawed out for dinner.

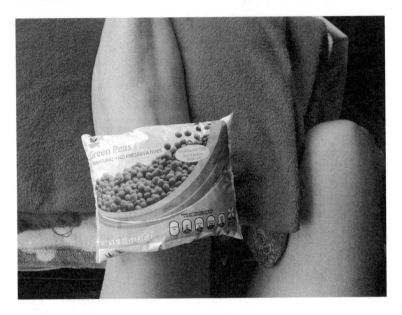

# Chapter 11: Social Hacks

Inanimate objects aren't the only things that are rich with tips and shortcuts. *People* are, too.

Herewith: Some of the most useful ways to get the most out of your social interactions.

------------------------------------------------------------

## The ultimate guide to remembering names

It's pretty embarrassing to forget somebody's name, isn't it?

If you met six people all at once, well, they'll usually cut you some slack. But if you've just met one or two people, and they're important—well, forgetting their names is panic-making.

Getting better at remembering names isn't rocket science; it's primarily about making it a priority. Usually, meeting someone is a chaotic blur of new information: Who these new people are, the new setting you're in, how they're perceiving *you*, and so on. You have to *remember* to remember names.

Once you've made up your mind, though, there are three tricks to remembering someone's name.

- **Easiest:** Say the person's name in your head at least three times, preferably while looking at him. "Harry. Harry. *Harry.*" You're creating new neural pathways in your brain that will make it easier to recall him later.

- **Better:** Say the person's name *out loud* a couple of times. Don't just say, "Hello!"—say "Nice to meet you, Charlotte!" And then again: "So Charlotte—what brings you to Apathetics Anonymous?"

  If you can find any excuse to *discuss* the person's name, you're golden. A little bit of "Are you a V-Steven or a PH-Stephen?" or "Do you write *Esmé* with a little accent on *e?*" works wonders for locking it into your memory.

- **When your happiness depends on it:** If it's worth even more effort to remember someone's name, make up a mnemonic—an association, based on the other person's appearance, clothing, background, hometown, and so on. People who remember your name *months* later do it this way.

  If his name is Rob, and he has a squarish face, say to yourself, "Rob the *Robot.* Rob the *Robot.*" If her name is Chloe, and she's from Cleveland, well, there ya go: "Chloe from *Cleveland.*" The sillier the image, the better you'll remember.

------------------------------------------------------------

# Helping other people remember names

Now suppose that someone *else* is being introduced to the group. That poor soul, having to remember five names before sitting down to dinner!

Remember the last time *you* were the new person, and you couldn't remember someone's name, how grateful you were that somebody *addressed* that person by name, so that you got another chance?

Great! Now *you* be that person. Use other people's names when you talk to them. "I *knew* you'd say that, Arnold!" "Pipe down, Randall." "Hey, Fiona, can you pass the salt?"

And it works the other way, too. Use the *new* person's name, to help everyone *else* out.

Each time, you're making the new member become even meltier with gratitude. —*Hitman616*

- - - - - - - - - - - - - - - - - - - - - - - - - - - - - - - - - - - - - - - - - - -

# Introducing two people whose names you're supposed to know

If you're supposed to introduce someone you *know* (say, your spouse) to someone whose name you've forgotten, you have only one way out: Clever phrasing.

Say to the forgotten person—"Hey, have you met Gertrude?"

At that point, if you're lucky, the two introduced parties will complete the transaction for you. Gertrude says, "Hello!"

And the forgotten person says, "Hi. I'm Esmé."

And now you know her name!

(If Gertrude is smart, she'll now say: "Do you write Esmé with a little accent on *e*?")

# What not to say when someone dies

You want to be a good person. You want to be helpful. You want to help soothe the grieving spouse, parent, child.

But there are only so many things a person can say—and a lot of them, frankly, don't actually provide any comfort. Some actually make things worse. For example:

- **"At least she lived a long life."** That's no consolation at all, and therefore a tad bit insensitive.

- **"Well, she's in a better place now"** or **"God works in mysterious ways."** What if the grieving person doesn't believe in heaven? Then that's a pretty hollow remark. Besides, that doesn't lessen the *bereaved* person's loss any.

- **"Well, thank goodness you still have other children."** No.

- **"I know how you must feel."** No, you really don't. It wasn't *your* loved one who died; it's almost arrogant to claim that you know how it feels.

- **"Well, be strong; your kids need you."** Oh, great. You're expecting the grieving person to feel even *worse,* because she's forgetting about her kids? You can't turn off your emotions; it doesn't work that way.

So if you're not supposed to say any of those common phrases, what *are* you supposed to say?

Say what you feel, and what you're willing to do. Make it better, not worse:

- **"I am so sorry for your loss."** That's true, isn't it? You can't go wrong.

- **"I'm here to help any way I can."** When you've just lost someone close to you, you're adrift. It can be an enormous relief when someone makes an offer to help—especially if it's specific, like, "Hey, I'm going to the grocery later. Can I bring you anything?"

- **"I remember how she used to…."** A brief, favorite memory. People tend to think that not mentioning the dead person is somehow helpful; actually, it's strange, and disturbing for everyone to avoid the subject. Offer to talk.

- **"How are you doing?"** Don't ask it the way you'd ask someone coming into the office. Ask it in a way that signifies you really want to know, that you truly care, that you're patient enough to listen to the answer.

Often, though, the most meaningful and understanding gesture is silence. Just showing up is already a wonderful gesture; a hug, a loving look, holding hands, being present and available for whatever conversation the grieving person feels up to.

------------------------------------------------

# The "stranger code word" for kid pickups

Imagine that you're supposed to pick up your kid from some activity—but you're delayed. You can dispatch a trustworthy friend, neighbor, or coworker to pick her up instead—but you've spent years teaching your child never to accept rides from strangers! What to do?

The time to think about this scenario is *now*, before it happens. Teach your child a code word or phrase: "lemon ice cream," "Barney's underpants," or whatever.

Then, if you ever have to send a substitute chauffeur, you'll tell him to introduce himself with that password, so that your offspring will know he's your authorized representative and not some slimy predator.

# Chapter 12:
# Life-Hack Lies

I f you were writing, say, a book on basic life shortcuts, you might be inclined to do a little research online.

And you would discover *thousands* of amazing-sounding "life hacks." How could so much magic be lurking right under your nose? "Cool! I didn't know that!" They're so juicy! We want to believe that they're real, so we keep passing them around.

But if you were writing that book on life shortcuts, you would, of course, have to *try out* those hacks to make sure they worked. And you'd quickly discover that a lot of them don't. They're snake oil. They're frauds.

Here, for your time-saving reference, are a few of the bogus ones that you can safely ignore—along with the number of times they appear on the Web, according to a Google search.

- - - - - - - - - - - - - - - - - - - - - - - - - - - - - - - - - - - - - - -

## To test a battery, see if it bounces (1,060,000 results)

D rop a battery from a height of 6 inches. If it falls right over, it's good. If it bounces a couple of times first, it's dead.

Wouldn't that be great? Sure. But it doesn't work. (You'll notice that in the YouTube videos of this trick, they're using different brands of batteries—that accounts for the difference in bounciness, not the health of the battery.)

# Rinse bacon in cold water before cooking (533,000 results)

According to this particular myth, if you rinse your bacon in cold water before frying it, the bacon will shrink 50 percent less.

It actually works—in your dreams.

*Rinsed*             *Not rinsed*

# Buy your plane ticket in your browser's Private mode (54,800,000 results)

You'll save money, because airline Web sites know if you're a return visitor. (They put a cookie—a small preferences file—on your computer to identify you.) So if you use your browser's Private or Incognito mode, the Web site won't be able to consult the cookie, and will assume that you're a new customer, worthy of favorable fares.

Only one problem: If you try this out, you'll discover there are no fare differences.

# To prevent a soda can from foaming over, tap the top a few times (525,000 results)

If you've shaken a carbonated can too much, the only thing that will calm it down is time. Try it yourself: Shake up two cans, tap one of them, and open them both. You'll discover that the tapping does absolutely nothing.

# To chill soda faster in the freezer, wrap it in wet paper towel (381,000 results)

Why would that make any difference? If anything, the soda will take *longer* to get cold, because the water (which is above freezing temperature) is a barrier between the cold air in the freezer and the can's surface.

---

# You can empty liquid faster if you hold the jug upside-down and swirl it (2,180,000 results)

Sounds like fun, but science is not on your side. A 1 gallon milk jug takes 13 seconds to dump out, whether you swirl it or just stand there and let it flow.

# Candles will burn longer if you keep them in the freezer for at least 3 hours before burning (365,000 results)

Nope. Makes absolutely no difference—and you risk cracking the candle.

# Acknowledgments

You've reached the end of the book. May at least a few of these ingenious tricks stick with you. May you sally forth with a renewed sense of confidence—or at least with less wasted money, time, and sweat.

Here are the delightful people who made this book possible.

At Flatiron Books: Jasmine Faustino, who made the experience wonderful, and publisher Bob Miller, who had the superb taste to decide to turn "Pogue's Basics" from a book into a series.

At the Levine Greenberg Rostan Literary Agency: my friend, and the world's best book agent, Jim Levine.

At TED: Chris Anderson and Bruno Giussani, who invited me to speak at the 2013 conference. My topic may sound familiar: "10 Tech Basics You Think Everybody Knows (But They Don't)."

Jan Carpenter and John Wynne stepped in to help me with the photography when the size of the task began to look hopeless. Julie Van Keuren, bless her, laid out this book—and cheerfully *kept* laying it out as I tinkered with its contents.

During this book's creation, I enjoyed the support and infinite patience of Jan Carpenter, Cindy Love, my team at Yahoo Tech, and my brilliant Brady Bunch of a brood: Kell, Tia, Jeff, Max, and Farley.

Above all, I owe a debt to my beautiful bride Nicki. Her love and encouragement carried this project all the way from, "You know what I should write someday?"—to the finished book in your hands.

# Index